**W9-BZG-553**

Thank You for Sharing

Other Books Published by the AA Grapevine, Inc.

THE LANGUAGE OF THE HEART

THE BEST OF THE GRAPEVINE, VOLUME 1

THE BEST OF THE GRAPEVINE, VOLUME 2

THE BEST OF THE GRAPEVINE, VOLUME 3

THE HOME GROUP: HEARTBEAT OF AA

AA AROUND THE WORLD

THE BEST OF BILL

In Spanish:

EL LENGUAJE DEL CORAZÓN

Thank You for Sharing

SIXTY YEARS OF LETTERS TO THE AA GRAPEVINE

THE AA GRAPEVINE, INC.
NEW YORK, NEW YORK
www.aagrapevine.org

Copyright © 2003 by The AA Grapevine, Inc., PO Box 1980,
Grand Central Station, New York, NY 10163-1980; all rights reserved.

May not be reprinted in full or in part, except short passages for purposes
of review or comment, without written permission of the publisher.

AA and Alcoholics Anonymous are registered trademarks of A.A.W.S., Inc.

ISBN 0-933685-44-0

AA PREAMBLE

Alcoholics Anonymous is a fellowship
of men and women who share their experience,
strength and hope with each other that
they may solve their common problem and help
others to recover from alcoholism.

The only requirement for membership is a desire
to stop drinking.

There are no dues or fees for AA membership;
we are self-supporting through our own contributions.

AA is not allied with any sect, denomination, politics,
organization or institution; does not wish to engage
in any controversy, neither endorses nor opposes
any causes.

Our primary purpose is to stay sober and help other
alcoholics to achieve sobriety.

CONTENTS

WELCOME

*I*magine a large and diverse group of sober alcoholics—women and men, believers and agnostics, old-timers and young people, free spirits and curmudgeons, country dwellers and city folk—and imagine them all sitting down in a big, comfortable living room, coffee cups in hand, and engaging in a lively conversation. What are they talking about? About Alcoholics Anonymous: what it means to them, how they use the AA program to lead better lives, what or who they believe their Higher Power to be, their concerns and hopes for the future of our Fellowship, practical matters and moments of spiritual insight. Imagine that, and you will get something of the feel of the voices in this book.

The Grapevine magazine, founded nine years after the Fellowship began, has been bringing AA sharing, insights, news, history, and individual viewpoints to readers for almost sixty years. Like the members of a vital home group, Grapevine writers don't always agree—in fact, they sometimes contradict each other. But what makes these voices "harmonize" into a greater chorus is love for AA.

If you're new to Alcoholics Anonymous or to the Grapevine, you'll find more information about both at the back of the book. Meanwhile, grab a cup of coffee and take a seat. Welcome to the Grapevine.

The Editors

Chapter 1

❖

AT MEETINGS

Experiencing Life and Sobriety at AA Meetings

Who would have thought that picking up coffee cups after a meeting would help us transform our lives? But going to an AA meeting is one of the great learning experiences of Alcoholics Anonymous. Meetings are living laboratories for the Twelve Steps and the Twelve Traditions. They teach us to listen, to get along with our fellows, to take responsibility for our own actions, to be patient, to give service, to ask for help, and to reach out to those who need help. They help us form lifelong friendships of true intimacy, connect with all manner of people, speak what's in our hearts, share solutions as well as dark days, and find a power greater than ourselves in our common goodness. For one hour or so, we can set aside our apartness and become part of a spiritual gathering with a spiritual goal. A lot happens in an AA meeting, as these letters show.

A New Truth

From Los Angeles, California:

OUR MEETING PLACE burned down last night. It was home to many of us, and now it's completely gone, except for a few blackened walls.

As I went to work this morning, I tried to pray only for knowledge of God's will for us. But the idea that our group could break up frightened me. Although I had no craving for alcohol or oblivion, I had very little peace of soul.

For four years I've loved this group and grown to understand the words, "*I* can't keep sober but *we* can." I did, too, and had just passed my fourth birthday—a wonderful, joyous day among good friends, old and new.

Then this unpredictable event—and gloom. A few telephone calls during the day to share my sorrow released my tension. (Good AA friends can share sorrow as well as experience, strength, and hope, I've found.)

When the working day was over, I wondered, now what? And do you suppose for one minute that our threatened group was defeated? Of course not. Everyone whom I've contacted by phone knows several available meeting places within a few blocks of our old meeting place. It's glorious, this whole adventure of a fresh start.

I'm rested now, and the truth is coming through to me: AA is not a place; it's an attitude of mind, a warmth of the heart—a spiritual fourth dimension where material things can't get the upper hand. It's where accidents and hardships and common problems draw us together just as surely as AA parties and conventions and birthdays.

Yes, we'll be all right, thank you.

D.C., May 1966

Listen—and Live Longer

From San Francisco, California:

MOST SOBER ALCOHOLICS have more than one reason for regular attendance at AA meetings. We all understand that steady meetings keep us away from the first drink. But there may be an entirely new fringe benefit to meetings where we sit and listen to other members share.

A recent article in a health magazine explains that the simple act of listening may actually lower blood pressure. After twenty years of research, the author had discovered that all communication influences our bodies. He believes that there are two parts to human language: the external language that people hear, and the language of the heart—the simultaneous internal "listening" of the body.

The postures and faces of AA members often express profound peace and comfort. In fact, the serenity, ease, and flexibility of so many members greatly attracted me to the Fellowship. Sometimes, the body can speak an eloquent language all its own.

I see and feel that in meetings. So coming to regular meetings of AA is a priceless experience for me on a great many levels—mental, spiritual, social, emotional, and now possibly physical. Listening quietly is already a joy to me, and if it calms me down and lowers my blood pressure in the process, that's just another great reason to keep coming back.

T.G., September 1985

There Is Always Something To Learn
From Oak Park, Illinois:

SPEAKERS IN OPEN MEETINGS are of many types and kinds, ranging all the way from bad to good, from short to long, from the stumbling and somewhat incoherent chap who is humbly trying in his own way to tell his story to the individual with the silver tongue using five-dollar words that flow without any apparent effort. All are trying to say something to help themselves or their listeners.

A while back, one of those stumbling, stuttering chaps made the usual remark that his thoughts were his own and if he could help someone else, he'd be happy; but on the other hand if there was nothing worth remembering in his talk, the audience would do well to listen because at least they could learn something about tolerance. Most of the audience forgot about the man and his tale and everything that went with him. I did not.

Sometime later I went to another open meeting and just listened—and found that listening wasn't such a bad thing after all. The habit grew until one day I was able to listen while an unhappy friend unloaded all his troubles onto my shoulders and into my listening ears. The man went away a bit relieved and I forgot what he said, only feeling better that I was in some way able to help a bit. With the maturing of the listening habit came sympathy, then understanding and that warm happiness that comes when one gets the feeling he can help, if not the other man, at least himself, because he has learned how to listen.

I have reached the conclusion that any person in AA can teach me something. All I have to do is keep my ears open and just listen.

H.S.O., December 1952

How Much Sobriety Is Enough Sobriety To Talk?
From Northampton, Massachusetts:

I STRONGLY DISAGREE with the idea that newcomers shouldn't be allowed to talk in meetings.

When I got sober eight years ago, a lot of things in my life came down around my ears, as happens with many newly sober people. The only place where I could talk about these things — and my struggle to stay sober in spite of them — was in meetings, and I did talk in many meetings during my first thirty days.

I'm not sure what my reaction would have been if I'd been told I wasn't allowed to say anything. Maybe I would have stayed, maybe not. In any case, I'm glad that none of the groups I went to were keeping track of lengths of sobriety and deciding who had "enough" sobriety to be allowed to talk.

Jody L., April 1995

Burning Desire?
From Rochester, New York:

WHEN I FIRST GOT SOBER, talking at meetings was very important to me. With a deep need to attract attention, plus a captive audience, the setting was perfect. I'd spout opinions, tell jokes, do almost anything except sing and dance. I flourished in an environment where newcomers were allowed, even encouraged, to speak.

Finally, however, it happened: An old-timer told me to shut up, to take the cotton out of my ears and put it in my mouth. I refused to do so and caused a scene at the end of the meeting.

Eight years have passed since that day. I still have the compulsion to speak at meetings, but I no longer have to obey every little compulsion that hits me. My latest burning desire is to share how important I think it is for me to shut up and listen. But I'd feel a little foolish going on about that particular pearl of wisdom, so I try to keep it to myself — even if it means white-knuckling it at times!

D.F., April 1993

The Quiet One
From Queens, New York:

I AM QUIET and do not mingle too well, but I do make friends and am able to talk to the people near me. I've been a member of AA for over a year. I remember so well going to a closed meeting with my sponsor and absolutely dreading it. After three months, I felt that everyone was waiting for me to say something. When my turn came, my hands perspired, my mind went blank, and all I could say was "I pass." I didn't celebrate my first anniversary, because I truly felt I couldn't speak, even though I wanted to. It was becoming an obsession with me. My sponsor, in her wisdom, told me, "Don't worry about it. Don't pick up that first drink and keep coming to meetings."

I find now that in my own home group, I am able to say something occasionally. We have a small beginners meeting, and that's where I've started opening up. I don't fret about this anymore. I am giving the problem to God.

A.K., August 1974

Tips On Talks
From Myrtle Point, Oregon:

I SOBERED UP in a large metropolitan area, where an emphasis is put on giving an entertaining talk. Recently, I moved to a small logging and ranching community. At my first meeting, I gave a fairly humble talk with a modest blend of irony, wit, paradox, and esoteric insights. The reaction, however, was shocking! The members didn't laugh once at my humorous remarks, nor did they seem to understand my profound comments. Stunned, I changed my timing and added more adjectives to my story in hopes of winning their smiles and applause. No use. They just sat there stone-faced.

In desperation, I finally came to understand that they just wanted me to share my experience, strength, and hope about God's grace in my life, one day at a time.

R.P., May 1977

No Dumping Here
From Belchertown, Massachusetts:

AN AA MEETING is not a dumping ground for negative feelings and personal "issues." Can a drunk hear the AA message in a meeting given over to such unrestricted "sharing"? Let's think about whether we're carrying the message — or the mess.

Abe S., May 1997

Afraid To Get Involved?

From South Lake Tahoe, California:

IT STARTED OUT like any other meeting. The chairperson spoke, and the subject of humility was chosen. At that point, a man passed out, landing face down on the floor. As two fellows got up to look at him, a voice from across the room said, "Oh, he's just drunk!" The two fellows went back and sat down, leaving the wet one on the floor. Three people talked on the subject of humility. The meeting continued as if the man on the floor didn't exist.

My mind flashed on the Big Book. Where does it say, He's drunk — don't get involved? I have a purpose today and that is to help the suffering alcoholic. So I raised my hand. I was shaking as I said, "This man on the floor is really bothering me!" At that point, as if I had given permission by acknowledging the drunk, four guys picked him up and carried him to a couch at the back of the room.

What's happened to AA? Do we need permission to step out from the crowd and show a kindness? Has someone rewritten the Big Book? If a man passed out in the street from lack of oxygen, someone would help him. But we don't help a man who passes out from a disease we all share? Let's not be afraid to get involved.

S.K., July 1985

Accepting Responsibility

From Leeds, Alabama:

A FEW MONTHS BEFORE sobering up, I showed up at a meeting intoxicated. I was loud and was being antisocial, and I was escorted out the door. After a short time, I walked back into the room, promising that I'd be quiet. But not long after, I erupted again, and the police were summoned. I was taken to jail, where I spent two days before being released.

If any drunk ever had a reason for not coming back to AA, I thought I did. But a month later, I returned to the same group. I accepted responsibility for my actions, made amends, and grew from the experience. So did the group.

If those folks hadn't taken the action that they did, I don't know if

I'd be sober today. It happened exactly as it was supposed to; I'm thankful for that now. I've since moved from that state, but I sincerely love and miss that group.

J.W., October 1992

The Gauntlet
From York, Maine:

WE RESERVE THE POSITION of greeter at my home group for newcomers who have a desire to get involved. With the customary turnover of newcomers, however, the position often goes unattended. And because I feel a need to greet people the way I was greeted when I first came in, I frequently fill in for the no-shows.

The function of the greeter is important: a cheerful how-do-you-do, a discreet question asking whether a person is visiting or attending for the first time, directions to the coffee pot or a meeting list, introductions to a long-time sober member. All of this made a huge difference to me when I was new, even though I was surly in response and mostly wanted to be left alone.

So it occurred to me recently, as I stood inside the building, that I was left playing second fiddle to a large group of sober drunks who were assembled at the building entrance—the smokers, who now comprise an unofficial greeting line. There is often a clot of people outside the door, mostly smoking and engaged entirely with one another. Greetings and waves are extended to familiar faces, but those who are unfamiliar pass through in silence.

Smokers have not volunteered to be greeters simply by choosing to smoke. Yet in an unfamiliar town, I have located meetings several times by finding a church or public building with a group of people standing at the door smoking. So I know the situation is not all negative. In fact, it can be very good.

However, there are several meetings in my area where, because I'm not known, I walk a gauntlet of strained unsmiling faces, many of whom turn away when I approach. Sometimes I see people purposely keeping their backs turned, and I hear them—totally unaware that anyone is in earshot, I'm sure—freely using four-letter words.

This kind of barroom behavior is understandable in people newly sober, smoking or not. But is this the way you want to greet people at your home group? Is this the impression of AA you want to leave with people who may be coming for their first meeting or visiting

from out of town? Do you think one elected greeter inside the building will balance this initial perception?

Whether you smoke or not, if you stand outside an AA meeting,
what you look and sound like will be one of the things that visitors
and newcomers will take away with them.

How do you look and sound to people who have to wade through
you when you stand around smoking and don't acknowledge them?
Might there be a better place to do this than the entryway to the
meeting hall?

What do you think—is it worth a business meeting to find a solution in the group conscience?

Anonymous, May 1995

Recognition
From Chappaqua, New York:

THIS YEAR, when I was on a business trip to New York City, I went
to an AA meeting of the Lenox Hill Group. As I entered, I was greeted by several AAs at the door. At once, one introduced me to another. I became a part of the group and no longer felt a stranger. The
evening stands out as a gem in my memory.

This idea of a welcoming committee is a great thing and worth
adoption by all groups. So many newcomers, or even strangers, are
reticent about talking to people; their shyness tends to isolate them.
A friendly greeting goes a long way toward combating this attitude.

Another point in the same theme is that many of us are apt to take
our older babies for granted once we have gotten them well-
launched. We neglect them for our new problem children and by so
doing, cause them anguish unintentionally. We forget that it takes the
novice a long period of time before he can build up enough assurance
and self-confidence to enter into the group spirit by himself.

This timidity, which so many have, is dangerous—it might easily
lead to wrong thinking or an eventual relapse. It's a frightening
thought that I might undo the good that has been done, by a simple
sin of omission, forgetting to say, "Hi ya, fella" to someone whose
very sobriety might hang on so little.

Isn't it something to think about—that happiness or tragedy might
just depend upon a slight sign of recognition, a nod of the head or
perhaps just a friendly smile?

F.V.G., December 1947

Lessons Learned

From Silver Spring, Maryland:

I AM A WOMAN ALCOHOLIC with children and a job. I've been sober in AA for over six years, and I've found a new life of serenity and peace of mind beyond my wildest dreams. A few months ago, however, I learned that a confidence I had given to one of our members five years ago had been broken; I had chosen the wrong person with whom to share my Fourth Step.

On another occasion my anonymity was broken by two AA members belonging to the same private club I belonged to—a club outside of AA.

As the result of these incidents, every bit of my serenity, humility, and tolerance disappeared. The resentment, intolerance, self-pity, and hurt that I felt were indescribably frightening. I was plunged into a state of depression and misery. I felt that my days in AA were at an end, since I had believed so sincerely that I belonged to a group dedicating itself to honesty and trustworthiness. Certainly I would be justified in never attending another meeting again.

Suddenly I knew that I was reverting to the old me: the one who consistently ran away when things seemed too hard to face. This I could not do. I also realized that I couldn't keep these resentments and hurts bottled up inside me for long lest I lose all I had gained through the years—and return to drinking.

In a state of desperation, I ran to AA for help, the only place I could go. I talked the whole thing out at a closed meeting. It was a revelation to find out that here indeed was the most loving Fellowship in the world. Almost everyone there played some part in helping me straighten out my thinking. They were forgetting themselves in an effort to help me.

This is what I learned at that eventful meeting. First, none of us is on this program every minute of every day of our lives. That is why we have meetings—to help us over these humps in life. Neither I nor the gossips were on the program at the moment.

Second, there is a certain percentage (small) of people in AA who are constitutionally incapable of facing themselves, who will remain dry but will never be sober. (Certainly when I came to this particular meeting that was the case for me.)

Third, I am in AA for a very selfish reason: to keep me and only me sober. I cannot afford to let myself be concerned with the other fellow's sobriety or how he maintains it. I cannot let anyone—not a single person in this world—rob me of my right to be sober. In other words, I must rise above these situations or I must die. But I cannot do this alone; I must have the help of AA.

Last, but not least, I had for a moment let myself forget all my friends and the wonderful help they had been giving me for years.

I am fine now, and, may I add, I feel a whole lot stronger than I did before this happened.

L.S., September 1960

Hold the Advice
Via E-mail:

ON THE QUESTION of whether certain topics such as sex or religion are appropriate for an AA meeting, here is my opinion.

If we work the Steps, we eventually get to Step Twelve, which tells us to take what we've learned and apply it to every aspect of our lives. Since questions and problems about such things as sex and religion are a part of my life, I think they are appropriate topics if they are "creating that disturbance" in an alcoholic's life that we are cautioned should be "calmed immediately." In many meetings I've attended, it's not the topic that's inappropriate, it's the responses from well-meaning members. Let me give an example.

Suppose an AA member is being pressured by a parent or significant other to adhere to a religion with which he or she is in conflict. The member is in turmoil and brings the topic to a meeting. If the chair relates the topic to a discussion of powerlessness over others or how we can manage anger or fear through a Fourth Step inventory, positive feedback can result. And it's always in good order for members to tell their own stories about how they used the Steps to handle similar conflicts.

If, on the other hand, members start advising this person about how to manage the relationship or how to stand up to "unacceptable behavior" in others, *et cetera*, then the meeting can quickly deteriorate into what I call a "Dear Abby" session.

The chair holds the key. By focusing, and if necessary refocusing, the discussion on the Steps and on personal experience, any topic can yield a wealth of good living tips.

Don C., May 2000

Time Spent
From Fort Myers, Florida:

I THINK THAT almost any problem can relate to alcoholism, and I don't object to a mention of these problems at an AA meeting—such as "I also used drugs when I was drinking." (I myself drank Nyquil and paregoric, although I never used street drugs.) I do object to a lengthy description of such a problem. When explicit details are given—for example, about using needles or buying drugs—and these details go on for five minutes or more, I think the person is then discussing drugs instead of alcoholism. The same applies to discussions of religion, sex, relationships, and so on. The greater the detail given, the fewer the people who can identify. In my opinion, it is not the subject, so much as the length of time spent on the subject, that's important.

Betty W., May 2000

A Distasteful Habit
From Quincy, Massachusetts:

I HAVE JUST RETURNED home from an AA meeting and feel rather hurt and somewhat taken aback at the adjectives, jokes, and illustrations used by some of the speakers to make a point. Profanity and smutty stories, to my way of thinking, are not only in bad taste but also entirely unnecessary in a decent program such as ours with an exceedingly strong spiritual backbone. Oh, I have my own stock of corny shady stories, but I feel in my heart that there is a time and place for them and it certainly isn't at my AA meetings.

As active drunks, our inhibitions were thrown overboard, and we acted and talked much the way we felt. However, now that we are in AA, and with the clear thinking that our sobriety has brought us, shouldn't we be able to control this one distasteful habit without too much of a struggle?

Arthur A., June 1957

Profanity and Piety
From Seattle, Washington:

WE'RE ALL DRUNKS, but we're also all individuals. Some of us would be more comfortable with profanity than piety and would be repelled by too much pious talk, and others of us feel just the opposite. Bill W. himself chased a lot of drunks away with his preaching. We all know many people who are foulmouthed and kindhearted, and others who are both kind-spoken and kindhearted. But, whether it's profane or pious, an AA meeting is a good place to be.

One never knows who may be offended by profanity. But no one is ever offended by another who uses his best words, not his worst.

Anonymous, November 1981

The Wrong Place?
From Canon City, Colorado:

THE INCREASING USE of obscenities is driving me from meetings. I go to a meeting to find a period of time where I can experience Tradition Two, and where I can feel safe from my ego—and other people's egos—as we explore solutions to our common problem. I don't think I'd be using obscene language if I truly believed I were in the presence of anyone's Higher Power. An occasional obscenity from someone struggling with hard times is very appropriate—I do it myself—but when people casually use obscenities for every part of speech, I feel like I'm in the wrong place with the wrong people.

I tend to believe that what comes out of our mouths is what comes into our lives. I can't afford to invite that kind of stuff back into my life. I was taught early in sobriety to stay out of toxic situations, but I never thought I'd find an AA meeting too toxic for me. For most of my seventeen years in the Fellowship, I've felt better on leaving a meeting than I did when I arrived.

I've often said that God and me alone aren't enough—I need meetings—and when a meeting turns obscene, my ego gets the upper hand. Increasingly I leave meetings struggling with resentment and frustration.

I don't think I'm the only person who feels this way, but my efforts to deal with this at the group level have not succeeded. I tend to think if a group is popular, what prevails at a group conscience meeting is what is comfortable for the majority—and our program doesn't succeed by doing what brings us comfort.

Wanda L., May 2000

Respectful Language
From Manhatttan Beach, California:

LAST YEAR, I HEARD an AA member talking about saying the "F" word in meetings. He said that he not only thought it was disrespectful to AA and the church we meet in, but also disrespectful to the women in the meeting. At first, I thought he was overreacting — after all, I'm a woman and this talk didn't offend me! No wonder — I was using that word regularly.

After taking my own inventory on this subject, I realized just how sour I sounded when I colored my speech with the "F" word. I thought about the fact that I might be the only example of the AA Big Book the minister of the church we use would see. Or the only example that one of the parishioners strolling through the church during our meeting might hear. And for the first time, I became consciously aware that I wasn't speaking in a way that supports anyone's highest good. I made a decision to cut that word out of my language and daily speaking as well.

I cherish the church I attend for morning AA meetings — it's over a hundred years old. The church council members are incredibly generous toward us. This morning meeting is held in a large, bright room and has a big kitchen, clean restrooms, and lovely grounds — I wouldn't want to lose the privilege of this AA meeting space.

For me, attending AA is a privilege, not a right, and I want to be a good example.

Ellen G., May 2000

Dump the Garbage
From Bullhead, Arizona:

I WAS A USER of garbage language: in prisons, in jails, in asylums, in military combat — and in AA meetings. Luckily, it was explained to me that I needed one hundred percent of the help, hope, and concern I could get from all AA members at all AA meetings. How much help could I expect from members who were shocked, bewildered, or alienated by my language? Not the one hundred percent help that I needed.

If I share my experience with you after a meeting, I say a prayer — not a prayer that you will clean up your language, simply a prayer that you won't resent my suggestion so much that your resentment will get you drunk.

My concern for your sobriety? Yes, you have one hundred percent of my concern. But that's probably not enough.

P.H., February 1978

Listening Heart-to-Heart

From San Francisco, California:

WHEN I RETURNED to AA in 1969, family, friends, job, and career were all gone. Being able to say just what I meant with a precise vocabulary was almost all I had left to be proud of. I wanted to find sobriety desperately in order to save my life, so I was shocked after a few meetings to have a couple of people ask whether I'd been to college, because I used such big words.

"Dear God," I prayed, "I'm asking these people to help save my life so I don't want them to think I'm stuck-up. Yet if I hesitate long enough to break down my natural way of talking in order to use smaller words—then my 'talking down' will shine through and be an insult to these wonderful people.

"Please let me speak from my heart, and please arrange the words so that they come out right!"

It seems that my Higher Power did just that. Now, my own ears don't hear street language when it's uttered, as I try to listen heart-to-heart. I love this explanation: "If the soprano's voice is flat, don't blame the song if it sounds awful."

R.C., April 1982

I Need Those Drunkalogs

From Monterey, California:

I LIKE DRUNKALOGS. I've had eight years of sobriety, and my need to identify myself as an alcoholic is as strong as ever. I find myself silently saying over and over during a pitch, "Yes, I did that, too. I felt just like that." I feel again the guilt and shame of remembering what I did the night before. I feel again the pain of a hangover. Then I return to the present, and I remember who and what I am—an ex-drunk grateful to be living one day at a time in AA.

I can get so spiritual that I forget where I came from. It would be easy to say to myself, "I don't belong here anymore. Surely, I belong at the feet of a guru, chanting to my Higher Power." Then someone gets up to tell how she puked all over herself at a party, and again I remember how it was with me. This spiritual creature would become a puking baby again after that first drink.

Recently, someone was talking about the beneficial effects of cream of mushroom soup on the morning after. Smiling and nodding my head, I remembered the many mornings when it took a tablespoon or two of cream of mushroom soup to let me know I would live.

Please give me the life-restoring spiritual pitches—but oh, how I need those drunkalogs!

G.M., November 1977

New Light on Forced Attendance
From Lakeside, California:

THIS MORNING, I FACED up to a long-standing resentment.

For a long time, many meetings in our area have been overwhelmed with people sent by the courts. Frequently, we were outnumbered by those who were hostile and resentful at having to be there. Often, I was one of the group members who were guilty of talking at them, instead of simply sharing experience, strength, and hope. The feeling of unity in our meetings was beginning to crumble. It was easy to excuse my intolerance by whipping out the old adage "AA is for those who want it, not for those who need it." It only served to reinforce my fear.

I was wrong in my attitude. I'd been jealous about AA and possessive of "my" meetings; the concern was for myself. When I asked myself this morning what I could do to change my attitude, I was suddenly overcome by a feeling of thankfulness for my sobriety, to the point of tears. I remembered that seven years ago this week, I was the defendant in an automobile-accident court case, being interrogated by a lawyer who kept asking me embarrassing questions about my drinking.

When I came into AA, I was told to look for the similarities and not the differences. It has taken me seven years to see that I prided myself on having come to AA willingly—whereas the truth is, I came out of desperation, just as most court cases come to us out of desperation, rather than go to jail or an honor camp. It took a lawyer to break down the initial pride that made me so resistant to asking for or receiving help. It has taken the ones who are sent here to help break down this last reservation of pride that tried to make me think I am different.

The old ways are changing, making way for the new—a new way of carrying the message to the alcoholic who still suffers.

M.L., August 1974

Small Is Beautiful
From Fresno, California:

RECENTLY, ONE OF OUR members had serious surgery and was unable to attend meetings. A few of us were privileged to take the meeting to her home every week—for *her* benefit, or so we thought.

I had become complacent, I realized; I had been in a rut. After eleven years in the Fellowship, I needed to have my enthusiasm for AA rejuvenated. Sharing with seven or eight people in a small meeting helped me to take a new inventory and discover that some of my old ways had crept back into my life: self-centeredness, intolerance, impatience, and confusion. I'll always remember those meetings and the lessons learned there.

C.G., February 1982

More Than Meetings
From Grand Island, Nebraska:

IF MY AA PROGRAM consisted only of meetings, I'm not sure I'd be sober today. My program of recovery must consist of meetings, talking to sponsors and other AAs, reading AA materials daily, taking time to visit with my Higher Power and listen for the response. I must have a life outside of AA and continue to use the principles of the program in all my affairs.

I believe that's what Bill and Dr. Bob envisioned for us when they designed this wonderful program. In the beginning of our sobriety we go to meetings and stay sober one day at a time, and that's about all we can handle. But there comes a time when we want to broaden our AA program and resume a life outside of AA.

Meetings are truly wonderful, and I attend two to four every week. But that accounts for perhaps six hours of my week; during the other one hundred and sixty-two hours, I'm able to live joyous and free, thanks to the AA program—including those meetings.

Betty P., July 1997

Cheating King Barleycorn
From Philadelphia, Pennsylvania:

ARE YOU GOING to a meeting tonight? Nothing could please King Barleycorn better than if you stay home. The disease persuades one man that he has a headache and keeps him from a meeting, and gets another to visit some old friends. The disease persuades a good many men and women to think they aren't feeling well enough to go out, although they will be at their businesses tomorrow even if they feel worse than they do tonight. The disease uses every weakness to help provide empty seats at the meetings: It's raining or too cold, too damp or too hot to venture out.

I'm going to a meeting tonight to cheat my disease out of an empty seat. If everybody goes, it will be a great meeting—with no empty seats!

B.G., October 1980

A Married AA Takes Inventory
From Alvin, Texas:

I HAVE RECENTLY been prompted to take inventory and evaluate the motivation behind my attendance at so many AA meetings.

Is it a fair certainty that I will be called upon to speak at the meeting? Will the miles to and from the meeting abound with the ego-building camaraderie centered around my AA "seniority" and vast wisdom about the program—while my Alateen daughter clears away the clutter of the evening meal, and my Al-Anon husband settles down alone with a book or the TV?

Do I, after all these years, really need x-number of meetings in a week more than my family needs me at home?

It strikes me that if I do need x-number of meetings, then I'm not working the program to top capacity, since the program is designed to equip me with the means to cope with my everyday living problems. Thus, the need for meetings should diminish as my proficiency with the Steps and the Slogans increases.

May I never put anything before the carrying of our AA message to a sick alcoholic, and may I always put the newcomer at the top-priority level. But perhaps it is time I took a good look through the inventory microscope and determine whether my motive in my frequent absence from home is need or ego or selfish pleasure.

N., November 1970

A Reasonable Reason
From Guam, Marshall Islands:

AMONG THE MANY excellent reasons for attending meetings is one that recently came to my mind. All of us in AA believe that attendance at meetings greatly assists us in maintaining our sobriety. We also know that going to a meeting requires some effort on our parts. Even though we may really enjoy the meeting, and afterward be glad that we came, there is still that effort on our parts to get there. After a day's work, perhaps we are tired and would like to stay home, or maybe there is a special show or program on for one night only that we would like to see or hear, maybe a card game, maybe a party. So it does take some physical effort and also an effort of will to forego these things and go to a meeting. (This does not mean, of course, neglecting to take care of urgent and important matters at home.)

Now, we all ask God, as we recognize him, to help us maintain sobriety. Do you believe it is right to ask for this help if we're not willing to make some effort or sacrifice on our own? Therefore, it seems very reasonable that we should at least put forth a little effort to attend meetings—if we ask for his help.

Leonard L., August 1954

Chapter 2

❖

YOUR MOVE: APRIL 1997

We Tread Inumerable Paths

*N*ovember 1996 saw two pieces published in the
Grapevine—"We Tread Innumerable Paths," an article by
June L., and "A Larger Welcome," a letter from Naomi D. —
which discussed the need for tolerance in the area of spiritual
belief. June L. wrote that she had recently moved to another
area and noticed that atheists were "being instructed to
pray or pretend belief. I think that shows disrespect to the
nonbeliever. . . . Instead, let's encourage them to find their
own interpretations of the Steps, Traditions, and other AA
advisements. [This] . . . adds strength to the Fellowship by
maintaining its universal character." Naomi D. regretted that
the 1996 General Service Conference had rejected the idea of
a pamphlet for the agnostic and hoped that "the
time had come to consider a larger welcome to
those drunks who have an initial or
ongoing dilemma with the concept
of a Higher Power." The outpouring
of letters that the Grapevine received
showed that this is indeed a vital
subject for AA members.

❖

Midwest Style
From St. Louis, Missouri:

MY FATHER MOVED to a retirement community in Arizona after several years of growing in AA in our hometown. AA was different in Arizona, and he didn't like the difference, so he stopped going, and after that he kept relapsing.

It wasn't until I was in AA, six years after his death, that I realized he could have started up a group for people who liked the Midwest style. I hope June will consider founding a meeting that handles the agnostic angle in the way that worked for her before. Others may well benefit from that option, too. In my own home group, believers feel free to talk about their personal conceptions of God, and nonbelievers feel free to talk about how the idea of God weirds them out. All are accepted because each is sharing his or her own truth.

Dan P.

Willingness Is the Key
From York Harbor, Maine:

MY THANKS TO JUNE L. for a good reminder. Whenever I hear someone being critical of AA—it's too much this or not enough that, or too many AAs do such and such and not enough do so and so—I remember how I felt about life in general before I became willing to join the Fellowship of AA.

Dropping out of the debating society, getting quiet with myself, striving for humility, developing some listening skills—none of this crossed my mind. I thought I'd be more comfortable in AA if only other people would learn to be reasonable and less superstitious in their approach to the program.

Experience has taught me it works better the other way around. When I focus on changing myself, I get better results. Trying to enlighten others about their lack of open-mindedness leaves me tense and lonely. "Live and Let Live" makes me happier with my life, my meetings, my friends.

Twelve Steps and Twelve Traditions tells us that "willingness is the key to understanding." It doesn't say God is the key; it says willingness. In my experience, the people who embrace this spiritual principle are demonstrably more open-minded, more emotionally resilient, and more contagiously hopeful than those who cling to a strict belief system, rational or otherwise.

So I've adopted many of the spiritual practices I hear about at meetings simply because, by being willing to try them, I've learned they work. For example: I still get peeved listening to AA speakers who are pie-eyed over some concept of a Higher Power that sounds more like Santa Clause or the Tooth Fairy. So I recite a mantra I learned at meetings: "Keep coming back." These words—usually intended for newcomers—are the best advice I can give myself. Real wisdom, I've learned, usually does bring me back to looking at myself. And I'm able to see that this experience of a great reality is something we all possess and struggle to express—regardless how each of us defines hope, intuition, awareness of a better world, a higher self, a pervasive wisdom in the natural world.

Call it whatever you want. Just keep coming. Don't drink. Ask for help. You will come to believe. If I did, anybody can.

Ernest S.

No Pressure
From Philadelphia, Pennsylvania:

I TRULY ENJOYED reading "We Tread Innumerable Paths." The religion of my parents was thrust upon me as a child. When, as a teenager, I chose a different denomination to worship in, my father physically threatened me. Shortly after that, I abandoned religion altogether and plunged headlong into my alcoholism. As an adult in recovery, I made numerous attempts to follow and believe in the faith of my family, and after each attempt I was left more confused and wanting.

Today I have a concept of a Higher Power that works for me. It is neither male nor female, nor does it talk to me or walk with me on the beach. I use the word "God" when speaking with others about it, because it's a word I think they can understand. This Higher Power expresses itself to me through my sponsor, the men that I sponsor, and others in and out of AA. Though it has no voice, I know I've heard its message.

I'm grateful that during my sixteen years of sobriety, I've never felt pressured to recognize anything other than my powerlessness over alcohol and the need for a power greater than myself to achieve sobriety.

Buddy S.

Getting Past the Second Step?
From Staten Island, New York:

JUNE L. SAYS that in the old days "we didn't discuss struggles with belief nor what God is really like nor . . . how God works in our lives if we let him." How can you get past the Second Step without such discussions? These statements seem to be based on the notion that sobriety is something we pull off on our own. If that's true, then why do we need AA? If I have the power to not drink, then why do I need any part of the AA program?

The term "God" was used by our co-founders Bill W. and Dr. Bob. It is a term for a deity that we are free to define on our own. The option to define his own deity allowed Bill to accept what Ebby offered him and allowed him to proceed along the road that eventually led to the meeting between the co-founders.

In the Big Book (page 12), Bill talks about his early aversion to God; he had certain prejudices to overcome and had met many people with the same struggle. After over one hundred people got and stayed sober, the Second Step became the distillation of their experiences with the God of their own understanding.

The section in which the article appears in the Grapevine is titled Along Spiritual Lines, yet the article makes not a single reference to the often-heard clarification that AA is spiritual, not religious. There is a vast difference between the two concepts. Purely religious folks would have the same complaints about AA as do the atheists. The notion of spirituality is where we can finally rest our hats.

I'm grateful for the opportunity to present my views and that June and I could share them.

Joe K.

Under a Big Tent
From Aurora, Illinois:

JUNE L. DEPLORES religious ritual pervading some AA groups. I'm in sympathy with the dilemma an atheist can face in AA. As a practicing agnostic in AA, I was early on disenchanted with the recital of the Lord's Prayer. Local AAs didn't hold hands back in 1959 and one could remain silent at prayer time without drawing furtive sideways glances.

Eventually I drifted back to drinking, and my alcoholism progressed until I suffered a nearly fatal binge. Returning to AA in 1978, I was astonished to find that pushy "God squads" prevailed in nearly every group.

Educated in science and mathematics, I subscribed to a view that anything that couldn't be counted or measured was meaningless. That kind of talk aroused religious proselytizers into making toilsome and snooty sermons. Since I loved contention, I used every opportunity to point out that alcoholic priests and clergy worshiped God to save their souls but had to come to AA to save their bacon, and that one's religion depended greatly on one's choice of parents.

The ensuing argle-bargles eventually helped me to see that my views were just as narrow-minded as those of the God squads. As I began to mellow, so did the sermonizers. Looking back, I like to think we both learned a great deal about respect for the opinions of others.

I now realize that my earlier standpoints were mainly a form of intellectual pride and that unmeasurable and unquantifiable phenomena play a major role in my life. I began to accept the notion of a Higher Power. Now I pray, but in a Christian or religious sense I remain agnostic.

If AA is to survive it must be a big tent under which tolerance for diversity is assured. My concern is that if AA becomes a religious movement, a forum for pop psychology, or a cure for all the addictions and sufferings of mankind, it will be "diversified" away from our tried and true Twelve Steps. My comment for June L. is, "It ain't easy."

Jack F.

This Is the Program
From Moline, Illinois:

I'VE NEVER FELT the need to write to the Grapevine until I read June L.'s article. I'd like to specifically address this statement: "After my long and mutually tolerant relationship with AA, I've been having increasing discomfort with a pervasive Christian influence and with Big Book fundamentalism."

Why do certain members within the Fellowship of AA continue to struggle with the fact that there's so much talk about God in AA? Why wouldn't there be? Of the Twelve Steps that are printed on pages 59 and 60 of my Big Book, God is mentioned in Steps Three, Five, Six, Seven, and Eleven. We're told: ". . . we deal with alcohol —

cunning, baffling, powerful! Without help it is too much for us. But there is One who has all power — that One is God. May you find Him now!" This is the message of Alcoholics Anonymous — not my opinion or anyone else's. Step Twelve suggests that we carry "this message to alcoholics, and to practice these principles in all our affairs."

I was an agnostic when I came to AA over four years ago. After two years of suffering and humiliation from my inability to stay sober, I "made a decision" to try AA's program instead of my interpretation of it. Now I've come to know the meaning of happy, joyous, and free. And I believe that is due to God's grace and the program of Alcoholics Anonymous. If that sounds like I'm testifying on salvation, so be it. That is my experience regarding alcoholism and recovery.

As to the concern that "in news articles about AA, the implication frequently is that AA is strongly religious," my response is simply, so what? Since when is AA concerned with the opinions of outsiders regarding our program of recovery? When I came to AA I was so concerned with what others thought or said that I couldn't function in life.

Today, I welcome the atheist and agnostic to AA. They have a right to believe and feel whatever they choose. Yet I'd ask for the same consideration and tolerance from them. When I share about my God and what he has done in my life, please don't be offended. That's my experience, strength, and hope. It's all I have to offer — that, and the program of Alcoholics Anonymous as outlined in the Big Book. And let us make no mistake on that issue. That is the program of Alcoholics Anonymous.

You are free to disagree or disregard any or all portions of this simple program. That's your choice. But if you cannot stay sober or have not found happiness, joy, and freedom outlined in chapter five of the Big Book, I offer this suggestion: "Rarely have we seen a person fail who has thoroughly followed our path. Those who do not recover are people who cannot or will not completely give themselves to this simple program . . . ."

John J.

The Spirit of the Life Raft
From Naples, Florida:

LET ME SAY to those atheists and agnostics who "trudge the Road of Happy Destiny" along with us "God people" that the most important thing to remember and practice is plain and simple sobriety. I don't recall meeting any member of AA anywhere who absolutely insisted that I worship the "God of the Preachers" as the only way to achieve successful sobriety one day at a time.

I've often wondered why those who philosophically and spiritually deny the existence of a Supreme Being persist in being so, well, "evangelistic" about it. Why fuss over something or someone that doesn't exist? But I certainly can understand and sympathize with anyone who feels that God is being shoved down his or her throat.

As the Big Book says, "we know only a little," and the Steps are only suggestions.

For myself, the Big Book is a wonderful, life-affirming book. But let us never forget we're all on this life raft together—whether we choose to pray or not.

Denny K.

The Only Requirement
From Lansdale, Pennsylvania:

I WAS GLAD to read Naomi D.'s letter, "A Larger Welcome." I too wished the General Service Conference had approved the creation of a pamphlet for the agnostic.

Before coming to AA, I enrolled in a treatment program consisting of weekly group therapy meetings. We were encouraged to attend AA meetings and I joined the Fellowship, but several of my fellow enrollees would have nothing to do with AA because of its "religious" orientation. These alcoholics were all atheists.

When I first came to AA, I was often told that agnosticism is not a barrier to recovery. Yet I'm now often told that because I'm agnostic, I'm too egocentric and self-willed to have lasting recovery, despite the fact that my recovery is continuing. I've even heard AA members flatly state that agnosticism and atheism are the result of self-will. These statements distressed me until I realized the truth.

Skepticism concerning self-will is essential for a recovering alcoholic whose reason has been poisoned by the toxicity of alcohol. That ability to reason has to be reeducated to survive and thrive without alcohol. This reeducation is continuous and can only be accomplished through ongoing self-examination, willingness to admit error, and consultation with a power greater than that of the alcoholic with the damaged reason.

Total abnegation of self-will is a requirement for religious conversion. It need not be a requirement for sobriety. Religious conversion is only one path to lasting sobriety, and it is not a universally
effective path, since true religious conversion such as that which
blessed Bill W. is relatively rare—in spite of what religious evangel-
ists ask us to believe.

Many of us have searched diligently, prayed earnestly, and listened carefully to those whose spiritual life is oriented toward religious concepts, only to be honestly unable to accept those principles
ourselves.

On the one hand, we face the requirement of rigorous honesty. We
cannot pretend to believe what we do not.

On the other hand, because we seek to repair our damaged self-
will instead of denying it completely, we're told that we will never
attain lasting sobriety. Yet agnostics and atheists do have the capacity to be honest and are achieving continuing sobriety through AA.

A good pamphlet for the agnostic, explaining the effectiveness of
the collective wisdom of those in the Fellowship who've searched
before us and found the guidance needed for the recovery and repair
of damaged reason, would greatly benefit not only the newcomer but
also those among us who misunderstand our dilemma.

Richard C.

Foundation for Surrender
From Wyckoff, New Jersey:

THANK YOU FOR PUBLISHING June L.'s article about the importance
of keeping AA "nonreligious."

When I was five years sober, I found myself living abroad with a
very limited choice of meetings. The largest group was run by a man
who told newcomers that the only way to get sober was to believe in
God. He completely ignored the Second Step discussion in the
"Twelve and Twelve" which suggests we need only accept a power
greater than ourselves as the foundation for surrender: ". . . AAs
tread innumerable paths in their quest for faith."

Although a believer in God, I was horrified at this man's attitude,
and I and another member started a more inclusive group. It kept me
sober and probably helped a few other alcoholics as well.

Now, thirteen years after that experience, I've evolved into what
some would call an evangelical Christian. I don't bring this into AA

meetings and here's why: My God wants the message of sobriety spread, and for many new AA members, and a number of others, the best way to do that is to leave him out of it, and concentrate on the Higher Power concept.

If the author of the article started a group for atheists, I'd be among the first to support it. My sobriety is the foundation for the rest of my life, including my faith, and I have AA to thank for it.

Anonymous

Chapter 3

❖

A NEW FREEDOM

Putting the AA Program into Action

*F*reedom from alcohol results in many other freedoms, which is why the Big Book says that if we work the Steps and put the AA program into action in our lives, we will know "a new freedom and a new happiness."

In the following chapter, AA members describe how they've found freedom from self-will, anger, and resentment, from the bondage of self, from despair and fear. These letter writers aren't theoretical; they talk about real encounters with people, events, and inner demons that led them to be more aware and more understanding. To paraphrase the proverb one writer quotes: Other people can give us knowledge, but wisdom is something we have to gain through personal experience.

❖

Accept or Analyze?
From Chicago, Illinois:

"IF YOU WANT SOBRIETY more than anything else in life, you can get it." This simple statement repeated with the monotony of a radio commercial was the starting point of my happiness.

When I was trying to get sober, the confusion that is the natural consequence of an alcoholic existence was intensified by my almost uncontrollable desire to analyze everything—every statement, reaction, and action that touched my life. I had to know. All would be simple if I could only know *why* I drank, *why* this had happened to me, *why* the AA program worked. The fact that I ended up more confused made no difference to me. I continued to try to analyze my problems, analyze AA, analyze God, and analyze analysis. My good AA friends offered help, but I blocked them with "Let me figure it out."

Periodically, drinking again became the most important thing in my life. It was more important than duty, honor, and soul. It was more important than my family—they were neglected while I drank away hours and days.

At last, forced to recognize that my problems were becoming progressively worse, I became willing to make sobriety the most important thing in my life.

I wanted sobriety more than a job that paid me an exceptional income but kept me so exhausted that I couldn't relax. I quit the job. I wanted sobriety more than fame or power so I quit fighting. And finally, I wanted sobriety more than knowledge so I quit analyzing. Out of my vocabulary went such words as psychiatric, neurotic, compulsion, complex, frustration, and all their ilk. They didn't belong to me. I had never studied to learn them. They merely confused me. I was ready to admit that I was just another drunk whose life was unmanageable. Now I could live a sober life.

But how does one do that?

I traded dependence on puny self for dependence on God. I traded resentment for understanding, fear for trust, selfishness for love. I traded dissatisfaction for hope, dishonesty for truth. I traded retaliation for amendment, taking for giving. I traded leaning upon others for serving others. I traded sectarian bigotry for tolerance.

Cynics claim they have found little hope or faith or charity in this dog-eat-dog world, and I had always agreed with them. I said I'd be a sucker to try to practice these virtues while others ran off with the fruits of my labors. But AA by example showed me that these qualities not only existed but were the fabric of which sobriety was made.

Sobriety has become for me an all-inclusive term. It means everything from not taking the first drink to enjoying the present twenty-four hours.

I learned that when I stopped trying to analyze AA or God I found both sobriety and a Higher Power. I also realized that I could easily have found sobriety and God by honestly saying, "God, I am so confused—please help me."

E.L., September 1946

Knowledge for the Taking
From Willimantic, Connecticut:

THERE IS AN OLD Chinese proverb that says, "Knowledge is obtained from others; wisdom we must acquire ourselves."

How perfectly this applies to the AA program. Simply for the taking, we have the knowledge we need, based on the experiences of the first one hundred members of AA. They set down in the Twelve Steps the mechanics of the operation of rehabilitation, as they had done it, and saved us the wear and tear of formulating a procedure. We know that it worked for them, so we know that it will work for us. Their knowledge, as obtained through the daily and weekly power of association in AA, gives us a positive and workable procedure.

However, if we do not acquire the wisdom to apply this knowledge, then we'll have fallen far short of our objective. If we are wise to the point of realizing that the First Step is but a stepping stone to a new way of life and that sobriety is only the beginning, then that wisdom will allow the other eleven Steps to seep into our way of living. We will gain freedom from fear and anxiety.

G.F.B., June 1952

Simple Kindness
From Oconomowoc, Wisconsin:

LEAVING MY CAR one Sunday morning at the old schoolhouse we use for meetings, I noticed a pickup truck parked some distance from the usual cluster of cars. The driver was a young man about thirty years old. We looked at each other and I waved. I started up the steps, then turned and walked back to the truck.

"Can I help you? Are you waiting for someone?"

With fright on his face, he answered, "They told me there's an Alcoholics Anonymous meeting here."

"Sure is," I said. I shook his hand and asked him to come with me.

We talked together for about ten minutes before the formal closed meeting began. Then, as is our group custom, we broke into small groups. He was asked to join the First Step group. An hour later, with some semblance of a smile, he said, "I'll be back. You helped me." And he has been back almost every week since.

Sound familiar? If not, it should.

Please, please try not to take your usual seat until that new scared person feels the warmth of your welcome.

Remember that in extending the hand of Alcoholics Anonymous, we survive.

F.J., July 1992

Tough Sponsors
From Casper, Wyoming:

I HAVE TWO SPONSORS, and they must be the most wonderful ones in the world. Both are old-timers and AA "fundamentalists." I know that I must change, and I want to desperately. But I'm still very stubborn and often fight with unbelievable strength and cunning to hold on to my old habits. My sponsors see through me immediately and are very tough on me. For this, I'm grateful. Many a time, they must want to throw me over, but still they persist, always telling me the truth, unwelcome as it may be.

It's not easy to be sponsors of this type. It often means dropping important things they are doing, so they may help me learn to pray, meditate, be honest, make out a shopping list, discipline my children, forgive my neighbor, or perhaps just enjoy my day. They are never too busy for me if I am willing to try it the AA way. They love me enough to make me uncomfortable and risk my anger, for they know that this is how I grow.

E.K., May 1976

How to Land a Whale
From Victoria, British Columbia:

I TRY TO PRACTICE tolerance in small ways, putting aside the little resentments, making light of that stealthy foe, self-pity, which will keep creeping in. I know if I succeed, then I'm more likely to beat that great big resentment which nothing has been able to pry from its roots deep in my soul.

Mental poison is just as dangerous as whiskey and very frequently the prelude to a drinking bout. God save me from the spiritual destroyers of self-pity and resentments just as surely as he may keep me from that first drink.

As I stay sober, I've come to prize my peace of mind and serenity above all else. I dread scenes, I dislike contentious subjects, and I even shun arguments that begin to show the slightest trace of acrimony. For, although I'm sober, I know full well I'm only one drink away from possible insanity. And the surest way to get there is to cultivate such bedmates as resentment and self-pity.

This wonderful way of life has so much to offer us besides just not drinking—happiness, health (mental and physical), security, companionship, knowledge, and many other priceless gifts. We truly get to know ourselves as never before if we honestly study that Fourth Step. This knowledge can eventually make us strong, if we ask for help in the right quarter.

I know I must try to look after the little things and then those big fish deep down will swim along, and before I know it I will land a Major Resentment or a Whale of Self-pity. In this way, I've gained some measure of tranquillity as well as a deep and abiding gratitude to AA and the Greater Power.

Jim A., February 1959

The Three-Month Milestone
From Flushing, New York:

I BELIEVE THAT three months in the group is enough to convince the newcomer that he has made a right choice.

By this time he has a fairly good knowledge of the mechanics of sobriety and has made considerable progress in the solution of our common problem.

Things are starting to shape up on all sides, tension decreases or disappears, home life becomes more attractive, even alluring, confidence returns, business relationships are better, and health improves.

The sum total of all these factors is a marked and somewhat strange feeling of well-being, bordering on exuberance (not necessarily youthful).

This is unquestionably the delightful and very desirable state that comes to nearly everyone in the group about this time.

During this period it is well to take stock of things, and above all not to become confused. The confidence that has returned, for instance, should not manifest itself in a way that spells arrogance. "Walking softly" is a fine art, not an act of subservience.

Nor is our sobriety our own exclusive attainment. Remember, all activities in AA are strictly a "we" not an "I" proposition; otherwise I could not have received any of the benefits that have accrued to me, for the group would have disappeared long before I found it.

It is also advisable to remember that an element of emotional ecstasy is likely to be present at this time; this will probably wear off. This should cause no concern, as there are many substitutes, depending on the individual's personality, tastes, and inclinations.

Above all, strive to recognize all forms of arrogance in yourself, "walk softly," and maintain a healthy interest in the group.

Frank L., January 1946

It Always Works!
From Newbury Park, California:

I WAS ATTENDING an AA meeting in an area I'd just moved into. During the coffee break, one of the men came over to me. After he'd said hello, he brusquely proceeded to ask me a series of questions about myself. Several people around me whispered, "That's __ __. He's not all there—stay away from him." I did stay away from him, rationalizing, "Well, I'm alone, unmarried, new here, I have to be careful, *etcetera.*" But something inside of me did not feel right about this decision.

A few months later, this very man led an AA speaker meeting and shared part of his story. Yes, he had in the past been institutionalized. But then neither had I come into AA because I'd been perfect all along!

I was overwhelmed at what he'd experienced, that he'd been able to recover and share his hope and strength with others. Going up to him at break time, I expressed my gratitude to him, saying that I felt his story was inspirational.

His face broke into a huge smile as he said, "Gee, thanks, I really appreciate you telling me that. Thanks!" Funny, at that moment I didn't see anything to fear at all—there was just a powerful, good feeling surrounding both of us.

Now every time I see this man, we greet each other with big smiles and a handclasp, and this always reminds me that when we let go and let God and practice these principles in all our affairs, that good feeling of love stays with us. AA is love—and it always works!

A.H., August 1986

Letters to the Editor
From Tampa, Florida:

HOW OFTEN A PERSON will go to a friend asking advice, while all the time he has definitely decided upon the course he will follow. Actually he is not seeking advice; he wants approval. We alcoholics have for years devoted a great deal of effort to changing rules to fit our actions. Whenever we could not or would not conform, we simply changed the rules.

Five years ago I made a decision to turn my will and my life over to the care of God. But often today, when I think I am asking God for advice, I am actually looking for what I want to do. I am still trying to change the rules to suit my actions.

Much to my surprise, after I went into AA, I found that I had not been trying to quit drinking; all my efforts were devoted to trying to learn to drink normally. Not until I really had a desire to quit did I have any success. A sincere desire for knowledge of God's will for me and the power to carry it out must be my daily prayer. A reluctant decision to live by God's will—as amended by myself—is not enough.

A good question to ask myself frequently is: What am I looking for—advice or approval?

Roy Y., May 1945

The Peace Process
From Gold River, California:

WHEN I WAS DRINKING, I thought I was the most patient and tolerant person in the world. And I was—as long as things went my way. Today, after nearly twenty years in AA, I know that my impatience and intolerance are symptoms of my self-will. The question is how to avoid getting trapped in the compelling pull of anger-based impatience and intolerance.

The Tenth Step offers immediate release from the bondage of self. Merely wanting to be patient and tolerant isn't enough. I have to develop the skill of the Tenth Step.

For me, asking God to remove the ill feeling works pretty well. But if my anger persists, I need to do more. A quick written inventory, using the approach taught in the Big Book, allows me to focus on the problem: me. At this point, I'm often cleared of the angry feeling. But unless I do more, there's a strong chance it will return. What then?

Step Ten instructs me to share my self-investigation with another alcoholic—immediately. This prevents me from rationalizing the problem and talking myself out of the next part of the Step—the prompt amends.

I've found that this angry feeling often persists until I make amends. Then and only then am I free. Once the entire Tenth Step process is completed, I'm at peace. And guess what? I become patient and tolerant.

Some people wonder what the presence of God feels like. I believe it feels like the peace I get from an effective Tenth Step.

Bruce T., December 1996

How To Make a Lifeline
From Grand Rapids, Michigan:

TO THE NEWCOMER in AA, it must be rather puzzling to hear the old-timers talk about their faith in AA, the meetings, the Twelve Steps, the Higher Power, *etcetera*. Usually, if the newcomer has been sober a week or so, and has attended only a few meetings, about all he's got is a faint hope that maybe he'll be able to stay on the wagon a little longer than the last time.

When I was a boy in Scotland, I worked in a jute mill. The jute came in bales from India and was brown, fibrous stuff, very fine, that pulled apart when picked up. It was dumped into a hopper with warm wax, rolled into threads, and wound around spools. It was still fragile; untwisted, the thread could be broken with a small tug. These spools were mounted on racks, and three or four of them were fed simultaneously into a twisting machine, then rolled onto a larger bobbin. This three- or four-ply twine was a bit tougher and had to be cut with a knife.

The process was repeated with larger twisting machines, until the end product was a rope or hawser strong enough to hold the Queen Mary to its berth in the fiercest of storms.

So, newcomers, bring your doubts and weak hopes to the hoppers—or meetings—to the twisting machines of the Twelve Steps and the warm wax of fellowship, and your sobriety line will soon be strong enough to withstand the storms of life. And we guarantee there will be no energy shortage from the Power greater than ourselves.

F.Q., September 1974

The Invisible Line
From Redwood City, California:

THIS IS ABOUT the idea "Don't quit five minutes before the miracle."

We in AA talk about crossing the invisible line into our alcoholism. What about crossing the invisible line into the program of Alcoholics Anonymous?

In my first year of sobriety, I fought to stay sober. It was the hardest thing in my life. I had so many new feelings. And what do you do when you know nothing else but to drink? I went to meetings and shared my feelings. There were days when I'd feel okay, and then the next day I'd want to drink.

Then, a year into my sobriety, the miracle happened. I was sitting in a meeting, and I said to myself, "Oh my God, I don't want to drink." I had crossed the invisible line into Alcoholics Anonymous! What a gift.

The same thing can happen to you. Don't quit five minutes before that miracle, when you cross the invisible line into AA.

L.L., April 1993

After Three Months
From New York, New York:

HERE ARE MY IMPRESSIONS of AA, after being a member for three months: Following a nine-month period of not drinking, during which I was most unhappy, I decided it would be possible to start drinking again, holding it under control. Strangely, I was encouraged by my friends who mistakenly insisted that I was not an alcoholic and should not be deprived of this pleasure.

For the next six months I seemed to be progressing satisfactorily—never taking more than two bottles of beer or a few glasses of wine each day. One evening, however, after this quota, I surreptitiously drained a small vestige of rum remaining in a bottle and almost immediately came the thought, "This is not so good!" Although I didn't realize it, after that action (AAs would say it was actually after that first bottle of beer), I was in danger. You see, I was a lone and secret drinker, the very worst of all.

From then on, the old habit reasserted itself, and while I was able to hold it within bounds of detection, I knew that wouldn't be possible for long. One day I had several small glasses of rum before going to work, and that terrified me.

After this I decided to seriously consider the AA program. I had attended meetings before but always with the mental reservation that I would not enroll myself until I was convinced I really needed it. I harbored the delusion that this habit could be controlled by intelligent analysis and willpower.

Several of the women members got in touch with me, but I was entirely unable to talk with them. Emotional conflicts were making it difficult for me to do anything except not take a drink. I found the open meetings more beneficial, for there I could sit quietly and try to understand what force prompted these speakers to express themselves so candidly and with such sincerity.

Although I am a person of no particular religious conviction, it gradually occurred to me that here I was finding access to a new philosophy of living, which is the essence of all religion. I have not tried to completely analyze the Twelve Steps or even the book. To me the three essentials are honesty, humility, and faith. Upon these I have set my standard, and I am making progress.

The oft-discussed personality change I have already experienced. Courage, through the help of God, has been granted me at a time when I need it most, to face a personal crisis. Humility has replaced arrogance and the desire for unselfish action has superseded egocentric proclivities.

I know there is a long way to go, for as I look back on my life I see it followed an alcoholic pattern from the very first drink. The opportunity to make amends for a sadly messed up life has come late, but I am immeasurably grateful that it came before total disintegration of a character and personality that once had potentiality for accomplishment.

An inscription on a wall at the American Museum of Natural History seems to me a most admirable expression of philosophical encouragement. I quote, in part:

Only they are fit to live,
Who do not fear to die,
Nor are they fit to die,
Who shrink from the joy of life
and the duty of life.

A.F., September 1945

What Happened to an AA Expert
From Marion, Indiana:

I WAS SOBER ten years, and I just couldn't accept the fact that I had to leave my great AA community in southern Florida. There was a lot of activity all the time, a big clubhouse, and plenty of meetings, and that was what I needed. I knew the little town in Indiana I was headed for had maybe one or two meetings a week. With my great knowledge of AA and the General Service Office and the workings of the program, I decided I would first have to get this handful of Indiana AAs educated.

When I arrived, I came on very strong about Florida AA and how everything was done there. It didn't take too long for me to build up a lot of resentment and hostility toward these people. They just didn't want to conform to my way of thinking. Our relations didn't improve, and I felt like running or just saying to hell with it. Thank God for my years of sobriety. One day, I took a good look at myself and what I was trying to do, and I didn't like it. I was trying to run the show, and because of that, I was being rejected.

I realized that AAs here were no different from any other AAs. I put Florida back in Florida, and I began to change myself. I tried to practice AA principles again and to carry the message.

I've been here over a year now, and I think small-town AA is pretty good. I have many friends. I work for AA and not against it. If I ever move again, I will surely not try to move AA with me. I'll just join the new group and go on from there.

P.C., May 1974

Perspectives on Twelfth Step Work
From Forest Hills, New York:

AFTER MORE THAN two years of Twelfth Step work, I believe that the chances of success depend very largely on the prospect. However, results are so unpredictable that I frequently find myself trying to spread a little light when the patient is not willing to take the First Step.

As we all know, most hangovers can be helped by a patient listener who will be consistently sympathetic and not too demanding. Many times the victim will agree to and promise almost anything in order to get what he wants at the minute, be it a last drink or some new arguments to use with those he has let down for the umpteenth time. We do run into—rarely—youngsters who are ready and able to accept the experience of older people, but for the most part, each Twelfth Step effort has to be tempered to suit the individual.

An ideal combination to find in a prospect would include a recent and mildly disastrous bender, problems that involve home and other obligations, and a socially minded and intelligent individual.

Conversely, the knottiest problems are personal pride, which shows up as an almost impenetrable reserve or else a species of belligerency, an unwillingness to face the issues and to tell the truth, plus the many fears, real or unreal, that follow excessive drinking.

Example is a powerful help and if the prospect can be brought in contact with a number of individuals whose fundamental characteristics are like his own and who have emerged from bondage, the prospect will see very quickly that others like him have succeeded. He is frequently aware of an unspoken challenge to do likewise. Some newcomers respond to a logical review of their lives and action together with definite suggestions for changing the pattern. Others, whose current despair offsets their ability to reason, respond to emotional prodding. The latter type frequently reacts favorably to a direct spiritual approach.

One of the most effective techniques I've heard is to picture the individual's life complicated by one new problem each time he goes on a binge—as against the vastly improved condition resulting from no new problems and the progress made by time and abstinence in clearing up old ones.

It is my belief that the key to success in Twelfth Step work is a humble realization that our efforts alone are of small avail and that the most we can contribute is a real sympathy for our distressed brother or sister, supplemented by our sure knowledge that God has all the tools needed to help every individual who earnestly seeks his aid.

M.A.C., September 1945

A Low-Mileage Big Book
From Ventura, California:

THE NIGHT AFTER MY TWELFTH AA birthday, I came home late and found a man sleeping on the ground in my parking space. I couldn't park without waking or injuring him, so I decided the simplest thing to do would be to park in an empty space allotted to another apartment.

When I came out the next morning, he was gone. But from a distance, I could see a book lying on the ground, among some other garbage he had left. As I got closer, I saw it was a Big Book, brand-new and unopened. I cleaned up the mess he'd made and tucked the Big Book away.

Later that night, I took it to a meeting where I shared about my birthday and told the story of finding the book. I ended by holding it up and saying, "So here we have a near-new, low-mileage copy of the Big Book, which can now belong to the first newcomer who says he wants it." A young man spoke up and the book became his.

There are many ways to pass it on.

M.H., July 1992

The First Realization
From Kent, Connecticut:

HARRY I. OF THE NEW YORK AA group is up here at the farm [High Watch]. Seeing he is here for two days, I am pumping him for all I can get out of him on AA. He has opened my eyes to a lot I never knew.

You would be surprised how I have been able to get over resentments of family and life in general. I now look at their side of a resentment instead of mine. In doing so, it lifts a great load off my chest and makes me see life more clearly. This being sorry for myself is one of the ways to sap up my normal outlook. To think straight today means that tomorrow, and all the other tomorrows, will take care of themselves. This is a great foundation for thinking clearly. I never should have left the hospital without coming up here afterward. I did not know of this place until too late.

I regret I messed up so much in the last few years, paying no attention to AA when AA could have made my life so simple to face instead of all the hell I have caused people and myself. I was trying to fight this thing by myself, which you can't do alone. I realize that it will take me a long time to get the whole program—but with what I have gotten in common sense from the staff here and about AA from Harry, along with talking to people about their problems and resentments, I will come out knowing myself better. I'll be able to face life with a more open mind and have an eye to judge myself.

I realize now what the trouble has been. I have wanted happiness and refused to work for it. I have held grudges and resentments that have warped my mind. I have not been tolerant and fair to others and through the AA program I have begun to see life as it might be, not as the way I have looked at it.

Joe, November 1944

A Fruitful Moment of Silence
From Atlantic Beach, Florida:

THE CUSTOM OF OBSERVING a moment of silence followed by the Serenity Prayer at the beginning of an AA meeting is widespread. Its primary purpose, of course, is to enable members to quiet their minds and focus on the situation at hand: the meeting.

This is exactly what I did for many years—pause and prepare for sharing. As the meeting progressed and I listened intently to the comments by the participating members, I'd weigh each one and consider whether I could identify or learn or even agree with what was being said.

But after a few years of this at my home group, listening to many of the same people, I gradually became aware that I was, in my thoughts, standing in judgment and criticism concerning several of the long-comers. John always uses so much profanity—how can this be a Higher Power speaking through someone? Then there's Mary— she always says the same thing ad infinitum. And Betty—her comments never reflect the true AA philosophy!

My attitude continued in this vein for a considerable period of time until one day I became aware of my conduct: After a number of Steps Four and Five over the past ten years, I still had outstanding defects in the areas of impatience and being judgmental.

I'd lived in the AA program long enough to know that once I identify a problem, immediate action is required. As I pondered this, it occurred to me that I had a convenient tool to use: At the point when we were asked to observe a moment of silence, I would pray that I'd remain open-minded to whatever anyone said. Who was I to question through whom messages were being sent?

Shortly after this, I expanded my prayer, and now as I bow my head and close my eyes, I quiet myself and focus by praying, "Dear God, keep me open-minded as I listen to my fellow members and make me prudent in whatever I have to say."

It works—and meetings are never boring anymore.

Warren C., July 1996

Unfinished Business
From Hamilton, Ohio:

A FRIEND OF MINE once said, "When I end the day with unfinished business, I end up dragging it into the next day with me. And I can't live one day at a time until I've dealt with yesterday."

When I remember to take a quick inventory and share it with another alcoholic, I can see my unfinished business. When I'm in the present, there's no fear, anxiety, resentment, or regret because those are things generated by dwelling on the past or the future. In the present there is only action to be taken or acceptance of the way things are.

Todd C., August 1997

Twelfth-Stepping the Twelfth-Stepper
From Ogaki, Japan:

I CAME INTO AA on a Twelfth Step call—one I *went* on! My sponsor-to-be, Phil, had met me five months earlier when he had to ride home with me from a party. I was loaded, so if he didn't fear for his life, he at least had a good idea about me being a drunk (he was sober two years at the time).

Like many of us, I had a "cover" who, I thought, drank more than I did. Bob was a real drunk. He didn't have a job and wasn't doing anything constructive except drinking—and everybody was talking about his drinking. I didn't think they were talking about me. I believed I was somewhat productive, and that made me better than Bob.

But Phil could see what I couldn't see. So he came to me about three months after that party and said, "You know, Steve, Bob has a drinking problem."

Well, he wasn't talking about me, so I said, "That's what everyone says. But why are you telling me?"

"I thought you might like to take him to a meeting."

"What kind of meeting?"

"AA," he said.

At that time I'd never heard of AA, had never heard of alcoholism, had never heard of Step One, let alone Step Twelve. "What's AA?" I asked.

"Alcoholics Anonymous."

I didn't like the sound of that very much, but he wasn't talking about me, he was talking about Bob, so I said, "If you want to take him to one of your meetings, be my guest."

Phil knew just what to say: "I thought you were his best friend — so I thought you should take him."

I realized that if I was drinking with some guy sixteen hours a day, I'd better say he was my friend. Furthermore, I knew that friends were supposed to help friends. So I went on my first Twelfth Step call: I gathered up Bob and we went to my first meeting.

That was on a cold winter's night in Cambridge, Massachusetts, over thirty-seven years ago. I pray I never forget it.

Steve K., February 1998

There's a Better Way
From Mashpee, Massachusetts:

LOW VOICES CAME through the curtains. Snatches of conversation filtered through, interspersed with medical terms and names of body parts. I was awaiting ambulatory surgery in the outpatient department of a small community hospital and I was alone. I'd brought old issues of news magazines to read, but they depicted the senseless horror of terrorist bombings and offered little comfort. I couldn't concentrate enough to read a book.

When I arrived at Alcoholics Anonymous, I thought I had no fears — a sense of impending doom, yes, but no fear. My Fourth Step, however, showed me that most of my character defects stemmed from fear. Now the fear started slowly creeping in from somewhere in my chest. Alcohol used to hit my stomach and radiate warmth out into my limbs. This fear was like a chilling tingle that prickled its way to my fingers and toes. I asked for a blanket. The thought came unbidden into my head: "Why don't I just leave?"

I still had an hour until surgery. No food, no water — no coffee!

The lack of coffee made me feel especially deprived and annoyed. "If this gets any worse," I thought, "I won't be able to stand it." I wanted to run, to scream, anything to abate the feelings.

Many times in sobriety I've caught myself saying, "I can't do this." Now when I hear myself, it's a clue: I don't have to do anything with fear. There's a better way. I can ask for help and get it. My realization this time came in the form of being able to ask myself, "Am I okay right at this moment?"

Getting myself into the present centers me. I've come to believe that God is taking care of me. The relief was swift as I realized I only had to get through the next hour, half-hour, or even ten minutes. It's a miracle how the process works.

I'm so grateful I have the tools of the AA program to bring me to the realization that a Power greater than myself is restoring me to sanity, and I'm in the care of the Higher Power. Being truly in the moment and believing that the next moments are out of my hands — this is the essence of spirituality for me.

Kathi S., July 1996

The Relief of Letting Go
From Barstow, California:

WHEN I WAS A KID, my father often took my brother and me on fishing trips to local lakes. I remember one particular trip to a lake in southern California when I was about nine years old. My father told us that this lake was extremely deep, so deep in fact that some people believed it had no bottom. My brother and I thought that my father might try to fool us, but we were quite adventurous so we devised a plan to go to the bottom.

We found the biggest rock we could carry and decided to jump into the lake with it in our arms. We took a deep breath and jumped in. As we sank further down into the water, it got darker and colder. Down, down, down we sank, holding tightly onto the rock. When we couldn't stand the discomfort of the cold water and lack of oxygen any longer, we let go of the rock. I'll always remember the relief of letting go, for I knew that warmth and oxygen were now on their way to me as I swam to the surface.

I remembered this event when, in sobriety, I was having a problem letting go of my self-will and allowing God's will into my life. A fellow AA member told me to "drop the rock." I immediately understood what he was saying: If I let go of self-will, the relief of God's will, like a breath of fresh air, can come into my life.

Donna S., August 1997

Don't Put It Off
From St. Paul, Minnesota:

HOW MANY TIMES while driving down the road do you check your instrument panel for speed, oil pressure, and water temperature? You depend on these to indicate a trouble-free journey or to warn you of mechanical danger. By the same token, I use the same continuous inventory through a sharpened conscience to warn me that some thought, word, or deed of mine is out of line. It is then up to me to correct it immediately.

This does not mean it's necessary to make a great show of apology. It is a simple thing if done immediately. Only when I put it off does a molehill become a mountain.

I think you will find that most of your wrongs are mental, the result of screwy thinking—that is, if you are actually making an honest attempt to live the program. It isn't likely that you are going to deliberately hurt someone else, give a show of physical immorality, or give in to the physical passions of hate, resentments, and intolerance. It is primarily your thinking . . . your attitude . . . that must be protected. Therein lies the source of your words and deeds.

"As a man thinketh, so is he" is a practical truth, not just so many words.

You can readily see that I am guilty of striving for perfection. I've got to. The whole AA program is an attempt at perfection. Sure, I fall short many times, and ever will it be so. It is a positive fact that I shall never attain that perfection, but in the attempt I have discovered a new zest for life, a new and more interesting battle every day, and the peace-giving knowledge that at least I am trying, something I never experienced before. I believe that man's value to himself is the sum total of his positive reaction to the little things in life.

E.G., October 1952

Dry-Tight Compartments
From Burlington, Iowa:

TO ME THE SECRET of keeping dry is not any special quality of willpower but lies in living in "dry-tight compartments." Just as an ocean liner can be shut off into watertight—"dry-tight"—compartments, we should shut the iron doors on the dead yesterdays as well as the unborn tomorrows. The load of tomorrow added to that of yesterday makes even the strongest falter. The only way I can possibly prepare for the future of sobriety is to concentrate with all my power, all my knowledge and enthusiasm, on keeping dry today. I try to remember that the Lord's Prayer teaches me to ask only for today's bread.

Today's bread is the only kind of bread I can possibly eat. We are all standing this very minute at the meeting place of two eternities, of the past and the future. I can't possibly live in either of those eternities even for a second, and by trying to do so I can wreck both my body and my mind.

So let us be content to live from morning until bedtime. "Anyone can carry this burden, however hard, until nightfall," wrote Robert Louis Stevenson. Anyone can do his work and keep sober, however hard, for one day—if he honestly wishes to do so. Today well-lived and sober makes every yesterday a dream of satisfaction and well-being, and every tomorrow a vision of hope. So let us shut the iron doors on the past and the future, and live in dry-tight compartments.

L.E.M., May 1952

A Study in Efficiency
From New York, New York:

I RECENTLY READ a book on personal time management, and I think its suggestions would prove valuable to anyone but me.

I began, as the book suggested, to set lifetime goals for myself. My choices: health and happiness. To insure that I was always using my time to achieve these objectives, the book further suggested that I always ask myself: "What is the most effective use of my time right now?"

I set to thinking about what I could do at that moment to insure my health and happiness. Maybe I should use any spare time to do pushups. Then again, there were some letters and checks I had to get out to creditors. If I didn't, I wouldn't be very happy after the first of the month. Or maybe I should . . .

My brain was becoming cluttered with this trivia when the thought struck me: I can most efficiently use my time right now by not drinking! Here I was, ignoring my alcoholism by mixing up my priorities. My number one lifetime goal is sobriety—a day at a time. By drinking too much too long, I lost control of my life; but every day that I'm sober, time is on my side.

J.J., April 1976

Recaptured Art
From Campbellton, New Brunswick:

WITH THE COMING OF INDUSTRY and trade on a large scale, people lost the sense of mutual need and mutual love. We became business-like and scientific, and our values came to be marked by the dollar and the bank balance. That is the tragedy of what we call progress.

Let's face it. We must trade in order to live; the dollar and the bank balance are important and necessary in the lives of all of us. But the precious human relations—face to face, heart to heart—got lost in the shuffle of new machines, new gadgets, new tools.

This change even found its way into our personal dealings so that we have come to say "I can't buy that idea" or "I can't use him." We barter personalities as we buy and sell houses, cars, and lawn mowers. To get along in the world we have to sell ourselves, along with our credentials and references.

Why do I mention these things? Simply this: in AA, afflicted men and women have recaptured the lost art of fellowship. We came together because we were in trouble. We leave our references and credentials at the door. We learn that we can recover from this trouble through the most powerful remedy in the world for sick souls— the face-to-face relation, respect for one another as human beings, and the right to live well as complete persons. We come together in the downright simple faith that every human being has a right to health in body, mind, and soul. Together, we continue to strive for these great blessings in the Fellowship of AA.

D.A.S., April 1952

One Minute at a Time
From Lincoln, Nebraska:

IT WASN'T UNTIL I had hit rock bottom in my drinking career that I finally learned to live for the moment. I was going through detoxification at a Midwest treatment center famous for bringing drunks down cold turkey. I had been drinking and popping pills for eighteen years. When they told me I was going to spend the next three days navigating on orange juice and hard candy, I had visions of insanity.

I knew I would have to accept my plight and turn my life over to the care of God. In the next few days, I learned something I had never known before: We must accept what we have now, not what we had or what we might have had. I learned to live for the life-giving orange juice and the sporadic moments of sleep that God saw fit to allow me.

To a newcomer in AA, staying away from a drink one day at a time may not be very easy. Many of us have had to endure sobriety five minutes at a time. When I was suffering from withdrawal, it was sixty seconds at a stretch. I prayed for God to deliver me through the next minute. Every time the second hand on my watch hit twelve, I would utter a short prayer of gratitude. The minutes got shorter, my prayers got longer, and even to my suffering mind, it was a joyous moment when I made it through twenty-four hours.

For the person who is having trouble living a day at a time, I might note that clock-watching isn't advisable. It has a tendency to prolong things. If time seems to drag, do something you ordinarily hate doing: Scrub the bathroom, iron shirts, weed the yard. I guarantee that you won't be too concerned about your pain if you're doing something you'd normally abhor doing. This may sound like cruel advice, but it is a proven method; and results are what count.

M.R., November 1977

By George
From Charlestown, Massachusetts:

I AM AN ALCOHOLIC FELLOW. I won't go into how booze ruined my life and health. I have been in sanitariums and state hospitals, and my mind has dreamed the thoughts of the damned. Now I am in state prison, the last stop, and I want you to know that the Twelve Steps can work in here.

Take me, for example. For eight years, probably twenty-five times, I've had intermittent diets of bread and water in solitary confinement. Once I did two years in segregation because of some trouble I had brought on myself, through my own stupidity.

I began to hate everyone and suspect my best friends of conniving against me. I was praying for the day when I could wreck society and all it stood for. I was so saturated with hate and bitterness that I was no longer human. I went off on long tantrums every once in a while and was sent to the nuthouse for a cure—or whatever you want to call it.

Then someone told me about the AAs, and strange as it may seem, it was an officer who told me. I laughed at this and thought how jerky a guy would have to be to attend an AA meeting. But out of curiosity I went to a meeting—and I have been going ever since. I pray morning and night on my knees. I even pray for the guys I hate. I say good morning to my fellow prisoners, and I can't understand the change in my attitude. I have been out of the hole going on three months and have had no trouble since, nor have I been insolent or fresh to any officer. Believe it or not, I love everyone in here. (Sure, I know what you are thinking—"This guy is soft.")

Well, if I'm soft, I hope that I stay this way. I am trying to live up to the Twelve Steps. I am a Catholic, so I can tell the priest all my secrets. I even spoke at meetings a couple of times. In closing, I ask that all you fellows here give the AAs a chance and I know that they will do for you what they have done for me. God bless you all.

George P., December 1955

The Joys of Service
From Port Moody, British Columbia:

MY HOME GROUP, Sober Sunday, works the phones on the twenty-sixth of each month at the Vancouver Intergroup. I like to be available on November 26 because that's my sobriety date. But I couldn't do it this year, on my fourteenth birthday, so I made myself available on Boxing Day [December 26] instead.

Halfway through the shift, I got a call from a lady whose first words to me were, "Thank God a real person answered the phone." (My first thought was to thank her for noticing that I'm a real person and to tell her I've been one for the last fourteen years.)

At first she was so upset that I couldn't understand her, and I asked her to take her time, which she did. She told me she'd just spent ninety days in a treatment center, and a family member had dropped her off at the airport. She'd gotten the time wrong and now she had to wait three hours for the next flight, and the lounge was looking good to her. She didn't know what she was going to do for the next three hours because she didn't want to get drunk since her family hadn't seen her sober in years, and now she was.

All the time she was telling me this, the scenario of Bill W. at the

Mayflower Hotel in Akron was going through my mind.

She said she was sorry for being so weak and having to phone me about something like this. But I told her she was strong for asking for help.

"How could I be strong by asking for help?"

"You're not drunk in the lounge right now, are you?" I said.

"You're right, I'm not" was her cheerful answer.

That made my year, and I hope it made hers.

If I hadn't worked the phones at the central office on Boxing Day, I wouldn't have gotten one of the best presents I've ever had — helping someone else stay sober.

G.W., February 1997

Wick-ed People
From North Hollywood, California:

LAST WEEK I ALMOST had a little trouble . . . in fact I was so close to taking a drink it wasn't funny.

But I didn't take that drink! Why? Maybe because I have quite a bit of AA under my belt.

After I had calmed down and realized that I'd succeeded in getting through my ordeal, it occurred to me that we alcoholics are like firecrackers. Yes, when we first go into AA we are firecrackers with short wicks and when those short wicks get lighted with resentment or self-pity or any of the things that cause us to go off on a tangent, it doesn't take long before we explode.

The longer we go to meetings, the longer the wick becomes. That may be why nothing happened when I almost had a little trouble. I had a long wick and I could see it burning and getting closer to me. I could see the explosion coming and was able to reach out and snip the burning wick — all because I had lots of AA meetings under my belt. Remember: The more meetings you go to, the longer the wick gets.

Anonymous, October 1955

It's Never Time to Retire
From San Mateo, California:

IN A RECENT ARTICLE about old-timers, there was a reference to a certain type of old-timer who becomes more and more inactive, until finally he "graduates." It is my humble opinion that the use of the word "graduate" is an error—disintegrate is more accurate.

According to my conception of AA's educational program, the individual AA is both student and teacher, for it is just as important to learn as it is to teach. However, AA makes no provisions for the teacher to retire or for the student to graduate. The AA who acquires enough knowledge of the program to graduate—doesn't!

Most of us readily admit that we owe AA a debt we can never repay. With this in mind, it is difficult for me to understand how anyone who is still capable of being active in AA can justify his decision to retire. The mere fact that we cannot fully repay an honest debt does not excuse us in the least from paying all we can.

If I were to ask God for a very special favor, I couldn't ask for anything finer than the privilege of paying off my debt up to my very last moment on this earth. Only then will I be able to say I have "made" the program.

D.S., June 1960

Cured

From California:

I WAS CURED. Three years later I found that there is no cure. I had forgotten I am an alcoholic.

Three years ago last March I came into AA in San Francisco—I was a merchant seaman just off a ship, who had spent several hundred dollars in bars instead of sending the money home to my wife.

The details of those few days are not necessary to this account; suffice it to say that after years of drinking, this was the time when I really hit rock bottom. I had been making promises to my wife to quit drinking ever since we had married, and I felt sure that this time it was too late; that she would never again put her trust in me.

I lay on my back in a cheap hotel room staring for hours at the water stains and cracks in the ceiling, trying to bring myself to face life again with the realization that I had lost the girl I loved so much. When I did walk into the AA office for the first time in my life, I was so choked up I could barely speak. I'll never forget how truly wonderful a feeling it was to find that there were people who would accept me and believe in me once more—me, who had let my wife and folks down so many times.

Miraculously, I was saved in time. My wife came out to San Francisco eventually, and instead of going back to sea, I got a job on a Bay tugboat where I could be home the same as if I worked ashore. And we had a son, now ten months old.

But I thought I was cured. I began to take my sobriety for granted. One night at a social gathering of friends, I was introduced to a drink called a shandygaff, half ginger ale and half beer. I thought I handled it pretty well and I began drinking it at home. I found it tasted better if I added less ginger ale.

Soon I was drinking beer alone and having a good time, making a fool of myself occasionally but getting by with it.

Then came an alcoholic evening at a friend's house. I was shocked back into the realization of what I'd learned the hard way three years before: that I was an alcoholic and would never be anything else. I knew that my life would continue to be one fouled-up mess after another if I didn't return to the sane life of total abstinence.

I'm glad now that I was shocked back to sensibility. I had forgotten Step Two: that there is a Power greater than myself upon which I must rely, that I can never take the responsibility myself to assume that I am cured.

I've learned once more that the decision as to whether I lead a life of repeated wrong steps and steady declination of reputation and character, or a life whereby I gain respect from others and consequently regain my own self-respect, boils down to the one choice: whether or not I take that first drink.

Once more I thank God and AA from the bottom of my heart. I no longer have to look at life in the distorted shapes it assumes from the bottom of the bottle. Living in close adherence to the Twelve Steps, I can once again lead a sane life and be respected as a man.

Anonymous, May 1957

Good Advice
From New York, New York:

(From a letter written by an AA member to a newcomer friend)
I HOPE BY NOW you are feeling better, more able to enjoy and derive the most that there is in life. Read a little if you wish, of course, but not just for distraction — an awful word generally, meaning escape from yourself, which you can't escape.

But may I make one suggestion? Wander off once in a while by yourself to some beautiful spot where you can be alone, and get to know yourself and God.

To know yourself is not done just by reviewing your "misdeeds"; they are not you. It is not done by studying your faults and weaknesses; they are not you. Your doubts, fears, and apprehensions, your immature cravings, your self-indulgence—these are not you. They are all committed by your physical body, guided by false instincts and imagination, instead of by your real self, which is the soul—the spirit within. That is where your conscience is, and your wisdom and your strength—which no one can hurt but you.

Get to know your real self, my dear, this nice fellow who so wants a chance to use your body, with its mind and imagination, for healthy, happy, useful things, integrating them so that the conflict within him can subside.

There, too, in your real self is God—not a remote Being but a constant and living presence all about us and within us. Go out in the woods alone, or on a hill, and just listen—a listening that is in itself a prayer—until you feel him, and at last can hear him in your heart.

Ask deep within you for this union of the real you and God, and you will receive it. Seek, and you will find it. There will be no room for anything but the wisdom, strength, and courage that is yours.

And do not leave God's presence behind you—your awareness of it. Keep that awareness with you, hold fast to it, in the deeper level of your being, while you carry on in the upper level the affairs of men.

And don't forget that laughter is one of God's greatest and most beneficent gifts to us. Laugh with him sometimes at yourself.

N. H., November 1946

Sobriety for Ourselves
From Philadelphia, Pennsylvania:

IN OCTOBER 1959, I pushed a button that changed my life. I rang the doorbell of the old intergroup office on St. James Street here in Philadelphia.

A slightly-built man, with pale blue eyes that seemed to look right through me, opened the door and asked, "Do you have a problem?"

I replied that I did.

He gave me a great big smile and said, "I'm just one drink away from a drunk myself. Come on in. Let's stay away from that one drink for one day at a time together."

When we got inside, I told Jack D. that my wife was the one who thought I had a drinking problem. He said, "That's too bad because you're never going to get sober as a sacrifice for her. At the first little argument you'll get drunk at her. This is a selfish program. Unless you want sobriety for yourself, you'll never get it." This was language I could understand.

Jack proceeded to tell me about the progression of alcoholism in his life. His honesty made me recognize the things I'd pushed deep down out of sight. I wanted to get his courage to face them in bright light. He promised I could do that if I asked God for help each day, attended meetings regularly, tried to practice the AA principles to the best of my ability, and kept in intimate association with fellow members.

I have come to believe that if I follow this program of enlightened self-interest one day at a time, it will not only keep me away from that first drink under any circumstances but also help me to unselfishly enjoy passing it on.

Marvin G., April 1998

An End and a Beginning
From Detroit, Michigan:

I'VE JUST BECOME a sponsor. Nothing new in my life—but owing to the lack of activity these past two years, it suddenly becomes new. It's as if my Higher Power got tired of hearing me give thanks for all my blessings and always asking him, "What can I do? Give me more knowledge of thy will, etc." Maybe he said, "All right, let's quit this talk of gratitude and show a little action." So he gave me Janie.

Looking at her this past week made my heart ache. I knew I was the one person in the store where I work who could help her. But I didn't know how to approach her. To get a private word with anyone is next to impossible, so my prayers were for the right time and place but most of all, for the right words.

It all happened just like that! And Janie was oh so ready and willing. I didn't mention a meeting in our first short talk yesterday, but later in the day she came over and said, "Florence, will you talk to me some more? Can we have coffee together in the morning?" I wasn't too sure she would be in, the way things were going—but she was, and we arranged to get a table off to ourselves.

So I'm taking her to my group's meeting tomorrow night. That will be the end of this story and the beginning of hers.

F.H., April 1970

Stranger than Fiction
From Philadelphia, Pennsylvania:

ALCOHOLICS ANONYMOUS is a Fellowship designed and administered by a bunch of ex-drunks whose only qualification for membership is that they can't hold their liquor, and don't want to learn how. It has no rules, no dues or fees, nothing that any sensible organization seems to require. At meetings, the speakers start on one subject, end up by talking about something entirely different, and conclude by saying, "I really don't know anything about the program, except that it works!"

The groups are always broke but always seem to have money. They are always losing members but always seem to grow. Members claim that AA is a selfish program but always seem to be doing things for others. Each group passes laws, rules, edicts, and pronounce-ments that everyone blithely ignores. Members who disagree with anything are privileged to walk out in a huff—only to return as if nothing had happened and be greeted accordingly.

Nothing is planned more than twenty-four hours ahead, yet great projects are born and survive magnificently. Nothing in Alcoholics Anonymous is "according to Hoyle." How can it survive? Perhaps because we have learned to laugh at ourselves. When God made man, he made laughter, too. Perhaps he is pleased with our efforts and makes everything right, no matter who pushes the wrong but-tons. Maybe he is pleased not with our perfections but with our sin-cerity. Maybe he is pleased because we are trying to be nobody but ourselves.

We don't know how, but it works.

E.H., July 1992

Chapter 4

❖

YOUR MOVE: DECEMBER 1996

Online AA

*H*ow AA members use the Internet to establish AA meetings was the subject of the Grapevine's May 1996 feature, "Online AA—A Report to Our Readers," a two-part section featuring an in-depth article and a roundtable discussion by members of online AA meetings. The letters received in response to this article formed another kind of roundtable discussion on the pros and cons of this new means of communicating.

The Grapevine magazine continues to bring news to its readers of the expansion of online AA meetings through its regular department, "AA in Cyberspace."

❖

Hearing the Language of the Heart
Via E-mail:

I LOOK TO online meetings as another enhancement to my continual sobriety. By no means are they replacements for face-to-face meetings, but because I'm legally deaf and assisted by two hearing aids, online meetings can offer something I can't get in face-to-face meetings: I don't have to worry about missing anything.

At present I haven't learned American Sign Language, and even if I did know it, my district has no signed meetings. Online meetings allow me to fully understand another AA's experience, strength, and hope—and I don't have to wonder whether I heard it correctly.

Michael M.

The Coffee Is Always On
From Toronto, Ontario:

IT'S SO COMFORTING to know that the coffee is always on through AA online and that sharing is available when one can't make it to a meeting. I usually go to my daily noon meeting, but for the next three weeks, due to a tight schedule, it will be difficult for me to attend regularly. If I can't replace my noon meetings with evening meetings, I know that the hand of AA is there through the Internet.

Claudia B.

Stay Tuned
From Lake Oswego, Oregon:

I VIEW MYSELF as a "traditionalist" as I relate to the Big Book, the Twelve Steps and Traditions, face-to-face meetings, service work, sponsorship, and "living the Steps," and I was a bit skeptical of this newfangled way of talking to another drunk.

But I must admit that online AA seems to be simply another tool in the kit which, if used properly, can keep the message alive and give the alcoholic one more way to combat the cunning and baffling disease we face. Online AA helps, not hinders, AA members in this effort. It doesn't violate any of the Traditions and can help a great many more than it will hurt.

I listen to a lot of tapes as well as read the Grapevine, so I have a variety of ways to stay "tuned in."

Eddie D.

Back Home Again
From Arlington Heights, Illinois:

I JUST CELEBRATED fifteen years of sobriety, and it was online meetings that got me to go back to face-to-face meetings. With five kids, I had a hectic schedule. I'd given up face-to-face meetings and was staying sober by keeping a conscious contact with my Higher Power and reading the Grapevine and the Big Book.

Thank God for AA online! I'm now in a wonderful online group called Sixpack (we were a "pack of six" but have grown) and am once again very active in my home group,

Barb M.

Cyberspace Is a Place
From Palo Alto, California:

SOME PEOPLE have expressed a concern that online meetings are exclusive and don't meet the requirement of the Third Tradition — that the *only* requirement for membership is a desire to stop drinking. Face-to-face meetings also have other "requirements." For example, I attend meetings in Palo Alto, California. This doesn't mean that Palo Alto meetings exclude someone who is in New York. When in Palo Alto, you can go to the meetings here. However, you have to be here to go to meetings here. That's a requirement.

Institutions have requirements too. To go to a Hospital and Institutions meeting in a locked-down facility, you have to be an inmate or be cleared by the institution. This doesn't mean these people are excluded from AA. It does mean they can't go into prisons that have this requirement to carry the message.

Cyberspace is a place too. True, to be in cyberspace you have to have access to a computer with a modem and a phone line. But that's no different than having to be in Palo Alto to go to meetings here.

Ralph W.

A Postcard to the World?
From St. Louis, Missouri:

A RECENT ARTICLE in my local newspaper discussed the apparent lack of privacy in e-mail transmissions and cited one commercial server's rather fluid policy on 1) reviewing correspondence the sender believed erased; 2) providing names to outside parties. Short of encrypting every message, every sender of e-mail sends a postcard for the world to see. If the newspaper article was accurate, then there's no anonymity online.

With the best will in the world, online meetings could only be considered open meetings, with the same status as a public information meeting, because meeting participants cannot guarantee anonymity individually or collectively. In face-to-face meetings I can at least guarantee that I'll respect the anonymity Traditions. While I'm glad that online services give us the opportunity to get a meeting whenever needed, I'd oppose affording recognition to an online meeting as an AA group because of the inherent conflict with our Traditions respecting anonymity.

Jeff T.

In Any Format
From Tacoma, Washington:

I SPENT ALMOST THREE YEARS in Alexandria, Egypt, and was registered as a Loner, receiving mail from people all over the world. I—and later another alcoholic—started a meeting in the downtown area and sat there two nights a week. Many of those nights I was alone. I would have loved to have had another way to communicate with other alcoholics. Today, back in the States, I work a long-commute, swing-shift job. This doesn't provide me with as many meetings as I want (and sometimes need), but God has given me what I need—other AA members on the Internet. Through online meetings, I've met and talked with some fantastic people. They've been there when I needed them, and I hope I've done the same for them.

Last night, I attended a face-to-face meeting and received my nine-year coin. I'm sober today by the grace of God and the program of Alcoholics Anonymous—in any format I can get it.

Barry H.

Bah, Humbug
From New Roseville, Michigan:

DURING THE PAST FIVE YEARS at my home group here, I've often heard it discussed that a Fourth Step should be a written inventory. The consensus is that writing makes an inventory more real, more honest, and gives us something to look back on and review when going on to making the Eighth Step list. Likewise, online meetings can be more honest and give me a way to open up more. I write better than I speak.

I'm thrilled that at any hour I can find someone to talk to. Twice this week, I've had tormented thoughts at three A.M. Do I have to phone and wake someone up for support? No, because other sober insomniacs are online, ready to help me make it through the night. I didn't want a drink, I just needed the loving support of the Fellowship. Knowing I can talk and apply the Steps to my chaotic thoughts and feelings at three A.M. makes a world of difference to me.

As to whether online meetings violate Traditions, I say, "Bah, humbug!" I can't go to a meeting in Pakistan today—does that make it not a real meeting? Online meetings are like any other—if you get there, you are welcome there.

Eve P.

Everything Old Is New Again
From Thunder Bay, Ontario:

MY MAIL COMES in the morning, so when the Grapevine gets here, I pour myself another cup of coffee and sit down with the magazine and have a meeting.

Speaking of meetings, a group of us have started a meeting by mail. Letter-writing may seem old-fashioned and extremely slow in today's high-tech world, but it does work. Not everyone can afford to own a computer and be online. But it's easy to make copies of letters and send them out.

Right now, there are five of us in the group, and we write once a month. Two women live in Stratford; another lives in South Porcupine, Ontario; the fourth lives in Whitehorse, Yukon Territory; and I'm here in Thunder Bay. I'm the only one fortunate enough to know the other four personally.

We're currently doing a Step a month. Each of us writes one letter and sends it to the other four in the group. For me, it's like catching an extra five meetings a month—the letter I write and the four I receive. When a letter arrives, I pour myself a cup of coffee and I sit down and have a meeting.

Our system isn't by any means perfect, nor is it as sophisticated as Internet meetings, but it is a fun and inexpensive way to carry and receive the message.

Sonia R.

Good News
From Edmonton, Alberta:

WHILE I'M ABLE to attend three or four face-to-face meetings weekly, I was pleased to read that alcoholics who live in remote areas of the world or are homebound in our own cities have access to twenty-four-hour meetings with all their Traditions. Just another simple way of staying sober and serene. In fact, I may even sneak off to an online meeting myself when something upsets my serenity, or my character defects prevent me from practicing the principles of the program in all my affairs. Thanks for the good news.

Karl H.

Don't Forget the Hugs
From Silver Spring, Maryland:

I'M A SENIOR and an old-timer and haven't had a drink for thirty-six years, for which I am deeply grateful to AA. I still find any change difficult, but I believe these computer-age meetings are like old-time AA in a way—e.g., being asked if you qualify and to give some of your drinking story. And online AA offers a variety of programs and a choice of meetings—how wonderful to have an AA connection anytime day or night! What a purpose it serves to those who are confined. Yes, I am sold on the idea.

It would be great to have a computer set up in my home but for now I'll continue reading the Grapevine and attending my face-to-face daytime meetings. I don't wander out at night anymore, so it truly would be a blessing to have a meeting online. Except for one thing: I would miss the hugs.

Eleanor B.

A Commendation
From St. Francis, Wisconsin:

IT SEEMS THAT online correspondence is similar to the Grapevine: It does for the AA computer buff what the Grapevine does for the AA reader—provides an extended and important meeting.

Anonymous

Chapter 5

❖

OUR PRIMARY PURPOSE

Protecting AA's Singleness of Purpose

There's an old saying about the fox and the hedgehog: The fox has many tricks while the hedgehog has only one—but it always works. That's the story of AA: Our Fellowship is effective because we are single-minded—our only purpose is to help drunks stay sober. In the words of the Big Book, we have escaped from "a common peril" and share "a common solution"; for this reason, we can connect with one another at the deepest possible level. This connection of one drunk sharing with another—this identification—is at the heart of AA. Because of it, AA has survived and grown since 1935, helping millions of alcoholics around the world to attain sobriety. The power and help that come from our primary purpose is the subject of these letters.

❖

Who Is the Loser?

From Mount Clemens, Michigan:

THE AA FELLOWSHIP saved my life. Without AA as Bill W. and Dr. Bob founded it, I would be dead today.

Like many of us, I become scared when the survival of AA is placed in jeopardy. I ask fellow members to stop trying to save the world, and let us be sure that our decisions have one main focus: to ensure the survival of the AA Fellowship as a whole.

The major controversy today is: Should nonalcoholic drug addicts be allowed into closed AA meetings? What happens if we decide to adhere to our Traditions and say no? 1) Narcotics Anonymous (NA) will grow; and 2) AA will survive.

What happens if we decide to ignore our Traditions and say yes? 1) NA will probably still grow; 2) the controversy will continue and the unity of AA will be lost; 3) many years down the line, nothing will prevent an AA member from saying, "Well, back in the nineteen-eighties we were able to help the drug addicts, so why not allow people into AA who are addicted to eating or gambling—or whatever? We can help them too!"

Who is the loser? Not you and I. Today we have the AA Fellowship with the Traditions still intact. The loser will be the still-suffering alcoholic of the future. Where will he turn for recovery tomorrow?

So throughout this controversy, let us never lose sight of the still-suffering alcoholic. Let us make sure that when he or she hits bottom, there will be a place to go for help, just as we had when we became sick and tired of being sick and tired.

M.P., September 1986

Dilution

From Los Angeles, California:

I AM A RECOVERING ALCOHOLIC; my sobriety date is March 28, 1979. It makes no difference whether I'm male or female, a celebrity, a non-smoker, a pilot, or a lawyer. I'm a person with an allergy of the body and an obsession of the mind who has lost the ability to control my drinking. I recovered by taking Steps One through Nine to the best of my ability, and I maintain that recovery one day at a time by living in Steps Ten, Eleven, and Twelve. I have had a spiritual awakening, achieving victory over alcohol by being willing to go to any lengths, and have been reborn. My relationship with God is right, and I'm the miracle in my life.

It seemed so simple twelve years ago. Today I live in a large metropolitan area where there are over 2,000 meetings to choose from. One meeting alone has over 1,000 people in attendance. And I've witnessed changes in AA that I view with disappointment, anger, and even alarm. I wonder where the old-timers have gone. I see alcoholics walking out of AA meetings as our common problem and common solution get lost in what seems like psychobabble and a mental health marathon. I have come to the conclusion that being in a henhouse doesn't make you a chicken—and being a warm body in an AA meeting does not make you a member of Alcoholics Anonymous.

I wonder why our singleness of purpose (recovery from alcoholism) is diluted by so much duality of identification. I am tired of folks discussing at length their problems other than alcohol, thus muddying the waters for alcoholics who are still finding their way to AA.

Recently, at a large meeting where I was the speaker, there was a group conscience vote that only alcoholics participate in an AA meeting. It would seem obvious, but there were dissenting votes! We seem to forget that basketball players don't ask to play in tennis matches with the excuse that it's all a sport.

It appears to me that it's time for alcoholics to start standing up for Alcoholics Anonymous or we'll really start falling for anything. Bill and Bob were on fire with a great idea in 1935, and it has worked perfectly for me and countless others. Stand up and speak! It begins with just one voice, and today I'll let it begin with me.

A.S., January 1992

A Program of Inclusion
From Atascadero, California:

MORE AND MORE YOUNG MEMBERS have come to AA because their drinking careers have been accelerated by drugs, yet we expect them to share only about alcohol. The puzzling thing is that the Big Book is loaded with references to drugs—from Bill W. and Dr. Bob all the way through.

On other topics, do we expect members whose spouses have just left or died, or who have lost their jobs or their houses, to come to a meeting and parrot, "This too shall pass"? Or can they talk about life on life's terms and how the Steps and the Fellowship have allowed them to maintain their sobriety through it all?

Sometimes at meetings you hear the "F" word in every sentence — nobody thinks a thing about it. But just mention the "J" word (Jesus), and ten people will walk out! What about "AA does not wish to engage in any controversy, neither endorses nor opposes any causes"? What about compassion, tolerance, and unity?

We're not a program of exclusion, we're a program of inclusion. Our single purpose is to stay sober and help other alcoholics to achieve sobriety — period! I'm going to keep coming back, and whatever you share is okay by me — even if you're whining.

Clyde M., May 2000

A Change of Heart
From Spokane, Washington:

I AM A TWENTY-FOUR-YEAR OLD AA member. I have always considered myself on the liberal side of many things, and AA is no exception.

When I first began hearing about what I considered rigid Big Book thumpers asking people not to stray too far from alcoholism in their sharing during meetings, it was one more thing to rebel against. It represented more of the old-time fundamentalism I abhorred in so many other areas of life.

This stage of "Whatever I've got to talk about — whatever is hurting me — I'll talk about in a meeting!" was about a year ago, during my first ninety days of sobriety. This was a time when I was fortunate enough to have a sponsor who reminded me that while I was perfectly entitled to my opinion, this was a subject that was better discussed by people with more experience in the program.

He had given me a stack of past Grapevines, which I read frequently to help with the restless times of my early sobriety. I never read a whole issue, and rarely did I even read two consecutive stories; I just picked, higgledy-piggledy, whatever sounded vaguely interesting. Out of all the Grapevine stories I read during the period, the only one I remember clearly was by a young person discussing singleness of purpose. The author described going to a meeting predominantly attended by other young members who shared freely about being dually-addicted and on any other "life issues." Then an older man entered anxiously and identified himself as a newcomer.

The old guy listened intently, but exited quickly afterward. The author shook the man's hand on the way out and asked how he liked the meeting. The man replied that he had enjoyed it, but he had never done any drugs. He didn't identify with many of the experiences he had heard discussed.

The author went on to describe his efforts to reassure the man that one needs only a desire to stop drinking, but found it difficult to reverse the initial impression left by the group.

After reading this, my puffed-up, anti-fundamentalist attitude shriveled; I was deeply saddened by the thought that because of my selfish need to talk about everything in my life, I might turn someone off who needed the AA message.

The longer I sincerely strive to grow in the AA program, one way I've found to meet my personal commitment to our singleness of purpose is to have a network of close friends with whom I can share those nonalcohol-related "life issues" — without putting newcomers in jeopardy of not being able to identify and possibly missing the help they need.

I've decided to avoid fanaticism at either end of the spectrum. Using the example of my home group, I hold personally dear to my heart our Third Tradition and adhere to it the best I can.

Thank you, Alcoholics Anonymous, for freedom to change my beliefs.

Scott B., October 1994

The Illness Is Inside
From Ypsilanti, Michigan:

THE DEBATE HAS CONTINUED recently about whether drug addicts should be allowed to attend AA meetings. It seems the greatest fear is that in order to accept such people, AA will be forced to change in a destructive way. I believe AA has already changed, and to attempt to resurrect some nostalgic image of "pure" AA will only divide and frustrate us all.

Over fourteen years ago, a kindly brother in the Fellowship took me to my first meeting. On that hot summer night, I sat among middle-class alcoholics, in my patched blue jeans, a beaded fringe pouch hanging from my belt and with hair to my waist. I had injected amphetamines, barbiturates, and heroin, taken LSD and marijuana almost daily, and — oh, yes, I drank. I knew that aside from watching

TV shows or movies depicting Haight-Ashbury, no one in that meeting had ever seen anyone quite like me. I sat in that meeting on my hands and attended dozens of meetings after that in the same frightened, confused, and nearly brainless state. After one year of recovery, the group had to assign me a sobriety date because I honestly couldn't remember when I'd stopped drinking.

Some of those people thought I shouldn't be there, but a group of old-timers ran interference for me (which I found out later). They weren't sure I was an alcoholic either, but they knew I was sick, and they feared I would die if I left the Fellowship. In that first year, those glorious drunks spoon-fed me AA in small, palatable doses. They walked me through much of that year with a compassion that certainly wasn't inspired by my unkempt, disoriented state.

After a couple of years, these AA members gently addressed my alcohol use, and I was surprised to remember blackouts, increasing tolerance for alcohol, and loss of control—in a word, alcoholism! My God, I was both an addict *and* an alcoholic.

Those wonderful members in my first year! I'm convinced that their love, support, and nonjudgmental direction built the foundation that has allowed me to have fourteen years of uninterrupted sobriety and a totally new way of life. I eventually cut my hair, got a job, got married, and have a wonderful family of my own. My days are charged with gratitude for sobriety and with love for AA.

But now the rumblings come: Should we ask "these people" to go elsewhere? Will they dilute the Fellowship? Things will change!

It's too late! Twenty years ago, if AA members were eating Valium or popping speed, few would challenge them. Today I think we'd question their sobriety date. Bill W. experimented with LSD, and though I wouldn't think it was a slip then, I sure would in 1986. Today in AA, a recovering alcoholic is expected to be free from all mood-altering chemicals, because we know that the illness is not alcohol; the illness is in the person. Drugs and booze weren't ultimately my problem—*I* was.

I fear these debates, even though, being dually addicted, I am safe from the person who might ask me to leave an AA table. I am an alcoholic today because the Fellowship allowed me to find that out— without hitting the streets again. I will live my entire life with the abiding warmth of those old-timers who gave me a chance, who weren't frightened by the ways in which I was different. They asked me if I had "a desire to stop drinking," and I said yes, and that was enough. I want to offer the same opportunity to my brothers or sisters who are still struggling.

J.B., September 1986

Unloading a Resentment
From Thousand Oaks, California:

I'M AN OLD-FASHIONED alcoholic. I have a physical allergy to alcohol coupled with a mental obsession. I have no other addictions. I try to keep an open mind when it comes to the dual problem of alcohol and drugs. However, last night at my favorite discussion meeting, I became fed up as the meeting was given over to pill problems. This sort of thing will keep away old-fashioned alcoholics, as well as people who must, for a legitimate physical reason, take medication given by an aware physician.

I finally said that I felt the meeting should get back to the AA program and the drinking problem, and that perhaps our newcomers were also old-fashioned alcoholics (it turned out they were). I ended up with a resentment because I hadn't said something earlier in the meeting.

I don't think the greater part of an AA meeting should be taken up by pill problems—if, indeed, any part of it should. I don't think AAs should advise people with pill problems. We should inform them of the danger of addiction and then send them on their way to Narcotics Anonymous, with a reminder to keep coming back to AA for drinking problems, but please to leave their pill addiction outside the door when they come to AA.

Thank you for helping me with this resentment.

J.T., July 1974

Upholding the Traditions
From Goffstown, New Hampshire:

AT ONE OF THE FIRST AA meetings I attended, a young man was asked to leave a closed Step meeting because he identified himself as an addict and not an alcoholic. I left that meeting very confused because I identified myself as an addict as well as an alcoholic. I felt that the group member who had asked the fellow to leave must certainly have done so due to his own personal prejudices toward drug addicts. I had no concept at the time of AA's singleness of purpose, that common bond of alcoholism, resulting in AA unity.

As time has gone on, and I've learned more about our Traditions, I understand just how important our singleness of purpose is. AA is filled with such diverse people that the only thing we could all have in common is that we are recovering alcoholics. It's the one thing that holds us together.

Somewhere along the road of my recovery, it became less important for me to identify myself as an addict. I know in my mind and in my heart that I am also addicted to drugs, but I now identify myself at meetings as simply "an alcoholic," reinforcing our common bond.

One night, I found myself in the same position as the man I'd resented when I was a newcomer. A young woman came to the closed meeting I was leading and identified herself only as an "addict." I looked around and saw that other group members had noticed this, just as I did, but I was the only one who went up to her at the end of the meeting. I asked the newcomer if she had a problem with alcohol and she replied that she didn't, but that she did have a problem with pills. I was hoping she would say, "Well, maybe I have a little problem with alcohol," so our conversation could end. But since she was certain that her problem didn't include alcohol, I explained to her about our singleness of purpose. I told her I too was a drug addict but also an alcoholic, that there were open meetings she was welcome to attend, and that there was another twelve-step program for her addiction.

She replied with something I hear often at meetings: "Yes, but an addiction is an addiction." I explained that we were "Alcoholics Anonymous" not "Addictions Anonymous," and that if she ever found she had a problem with alcohol she was welcome to come back to our meeting.

The young woman left and has not been back. It's not easy to tell a person they don't qualify to be in an AA meeting, but I know I did the right thing by upholding our Traditions. I am responsible for ensuring that my group follows the Traditions of our Fellowship. They are there for our protection.

I was really surprised at how many of my fellow group members were either apathetic to the situation or thought the woman should have been allowed to stay at the meeting. If we had allowed her to stay, we would have ended up with a group of diversified people with no common bond. If she could stay, then anyone could stay.

I knew at that moment why the young man was asked to leave that meeting early in my sobriety.

Sue F., October 1994

Our Drinking Was But a Symptom
From White Pigeon, Michigan:

WE ARE TOLD IN AA that drinking is but a symptom of deeper-lying problems.

After voluntarily admitting myself to treatment twice, and finally being sent by the law, I finally realized over a period of about ten years that alcohol was not my problem. Alcohol was my "solution."

Each time I got ready to do a Fourth Step, I would back off. I couldn't or wouldn't admit that I was a human being and subject to all sorts of character defects. Finally, however, I did take the Fourth Step and realized that my problems were resentment, anger, jealousy, self-pity, and remorse. When one or more of these bothered me, my solution, although temporary, was to drink.

Alcohol was my drug of choice. But from talking to dually-addicted friends, I have discovered that the deeper-lying problems are the same.

Should we let the people addicted to drugs other than alcohol into closed AA meetings? I think so. We also need to offer hope that there is a solution through Narcotics Anonymous—or whatever program applies. We need to give the strength from our own experience and relate, if we can, to their feelings.

For this I am responsible, and also thankful that I can help.

H.B., September 1986

The Good of the Group
From Hopewell Junction, New York:

ABOUT FOUR YEARS AGO, when I was nineteen years old, I entered AA after being in two psychiatric centers and one treatment facility. I was placed in treatment after my last drunk, which resulted in a suicide attempt. I guess you could say I was at the jumping-off place.

I was blessed with a wonderful home group and a sponsor. Both helped me to see my alcoholism very clearly. As we know, there are a lot of other problems and addictions out there. I had experienced many. However, alcohol is what brought me to my knees. I thank God today for the fact that my group and sponsor loved me enough to tell me that I had to keep the focus on my drinking. I was told very quickly that the primary purpose of an AA meeting is to share experience, strength, and hope, not to dump my garbage. Right away I was being pointed away from the self-centeredness that ran my life when I was an active drunk.

Later on I had the privilege of learning about the Traditions. These Traditions taught me to put my personal desires aside for the good of AA and my group. This meant I should refrain from sharing at the group level on subjects not related to alcoholism, even the things I thought were so important to me.

I know today that it's only because I am sober that I am able to work on any other "issues" I might have. However, I go to the appropriate places for them; I love AA too much to expect anything from AA other than sobriety—freedom from alcohol. That, in itself, is more than I could have dreamed of.

D.M., October 1994

The Path to Sobriety
From Davidsonville, Maryland:

WHEN I CAME into the Fellowship of Alcoholics Anonymous at the age of eighteen, I didn't know what singleness of purpose was. Come to think of it, the only thing I knew was how to get drunk. I was scared, lonely, and didn't know what to expect. But people in AA started to give me hope that I could stay sober. It was hard to believe that these people wanted to help me and didn't want anything in return.

AA members who were ten, twenty years older than myself would take me out with them for ice cream or coffee after the meeting. Believe it or not, I had just as much fun with these older guys as I did with guys my own age. They showed me the path to sobriety and convinced me that I was worth something in the world.

Now, five years later, it's my job to keep our singleness of purpose alive. The way I see it, singleness of purpose is to carry the message to the still-suffering alcoholic who needs help as I needed help.

I remember being in a meeting after my first anniversary and seeing this guy come in with a Mohawk hairdo, a ripped shirt, and raggedy jeans. I said to myself, This guy is never going to make it. As the meeting went on, I was still judging him in my head. When the meeting ended, I started feeling guilty for what I was thinking about this guy whom I didn't even know. What would have happened if people had judged me and not given me a chance? Would I be here today or would I still be getting drunk?

I can't honestly answer that question, but I can tell you I stopped judging that newcomer and introduced myself to him instead. From that day on, we have been best friends, and I was able to help him as people helped me in the beginning.

So I always need to remember AA's singleness of purpose and have my hand out for the next person.

Dennis T., October 1994

Let's Stay Simple
From Detroit, Michigan:

IS AA GOING "the way of all flesh"? I begin to think so when I read in the Grapevine of AA buttons, pins, banners, and all of the other doodads—the kind that distinguish the great-orders-of-this-or-that, the ladies' sewing circles, the dinner clubs, and the push-the-hometown boosters. I'm not taking a crack at those groups. They have their place, and some of them do a grand job in civic and social enterprises.

But I thought AA was different. And then I read about and see the formation of committees for this and committees for that, and boards and councils, and heaven knows what. Just like the board of directors. Squabbles, of course, follow. Cliques appear and the old, ugly head of politics rises up.

Can't we stay simple? No matter how large AA becomes in its totals, we can still stick to small groups—except for the occasional large, open meeting held mainly to show the public what AA has to offer. It was in the small, intimate, personal relationship that AA began. That is still the way AA works best, in my opinion. And that's the way to avoid all of the organization with all of its attendant evils. Please let's stay simple, basic, fundamental—let's stay AA.

O.R., February 1948

Stop the War!
From Torrance, California:

I'VE WEATHERED many storms in AA during my twelve years of sobriety, and we in southern California have fought many battles. Our experiences with keeping to our primary purpose may help others.

The manner in which this problem is handled at some meetings in our area may not be a perfect answer, but it is practical and it works. A statement is read before the meeting starts: "This is an open meeting of Alcoholics Anonymous. All are welcome, but we request that only alcoholics share." The dually-addicted person can talk about his alcohol problem only.

Should a new person come to the meeting with a problem that isn't related to alcohol, he is directed to those of us who are dually-addicted. We can talk his language and direct him to another twelve-step program where he will find warm acceptance. Should no other meeting exist in a particular locale, one can be started then and there. (California leads the world, I think, in the abundance of anonymous programs for gamblers, narcotics addicts, cocaine addicts, *et cetera*). If there is no one to help the nonalcoholic newcomer, we permit him to attend the meeting but not to share.

AA cannot be all things to all people. But I must be of maximum help to anyone I can.

There is a simple answer to the problem of people who are dually addicted: Our Third Tradition makes AA an inclusive, not exclusive, organization. Our founders knew what they were doing.

D.H., September 1986

Pushing Old-Timers Away
From Chattanooga, Tennessee:

I WANT TO SHARE an experience I had at a noon meeting the other day. The topic was "Our primary purpose is to stay sober and help other alcoholics to achieve sobriety." We had made our way around most of the room when a woman in the back, who expressed no "identifier," shared about general recovery stuff. Two speakers later, a woman — not identifying herself as an alcoholic or even an addict — recounted her recent hospitalization for bulimia and how the meetings had helped her so much. The next speaker identified herself as being "addicted to relationships" and shared at length about her struggles. While she was speaking, I noticed an old-timer get up and leave the meeting.

Perhaps the two were unrelated, but I doubt it.

I'm glad that the bulimic is recovering and that AA meetings are helpful, but I think we weaken our AA program when no regard is paid to the Traditions. AA is in danger of becoming the parody that is laughed at on "Saturday Night Live." That scares me.

Although I have faith that our Higher Power will look out for us, I also know that sometimes I don't speak up for fear of being considered a bleeding deacon. We all have only one day, but it is the example and wisdom of the people who've been doing this for some time that helps give AA its much-needed balance.

Providing a place for bulimics and people "addicted to relationships"—while pushing old-timers away—is not good for AA.

G.G., October 1994

Opening the Door
From Eureka, Kansas:

PEOPLE IN MY AREA are talking about the Traditions—especially Three and Five—and gratitude for a Fellowship without stringent membership rules is being expressed. Thank God AA welcomes us with open arms and tolerance until we come to believe this is where we belong. I need to remember that closing our doors to someone out of fear that his or her addiction is the wrong kind might be condemning that person to death. Communicating in the language of the heart and applying the Twelve Steps and Twelve Traditions has kept AA alive and growing for more than fifty years. May we never stifle that.

V.F., September 1986

AA Does Work
From Farmingdale, New Jersey:

I CAME INTO the Fellowship when I was sixteen; I'm now twenty-two. I am very grateful for Alcoholics Anonymous. It saved my life and the lives of many others, and I am a firm believer that there is only one program of recovery—and that is the Twelve Steps and Twelve Traditions of AA. I cringe when people say there are as many ways to work the program as there are people in it. The program is written very simply in the Big Book and outlined in the "Twelve and Twelve." Our purpose is very clear.

But I often go to meetings where I wonder whether I'm at an AA meeting or a therapy session. As a member of AA, it is my responsibility to say something when a meeting is drifting. It says in Step Nine, "Let's not talk prudence while practicing evasion." Therefore I try not to complain; rather I try to be an example.

What scares me is the fact that I've heard old-timers say, "I don't go to a lot of meetings anymore. AA has changed." I believe one reason AA is losing its singleness of purpose at the meetings is because the more experienced members aren't showing up—or speaking up.

My home group meeting was having a lot of trouble a year ago. What was once a thriving meeting had faded almost into nothing. The group had stopped having regular business meetings. At that time I had to make a choice: Do I change my home group or do I stand up for AA?

I'm happy to say I did make a stand—not a power-driven stand, however. Rather, I took the secretary job and started practicing the Traditions. The group healed itself. AA does work.

It's not the people who are coming in now who are damaging our singleness of purpose. It's the people who have stopped coming who do the real damage. It's too easy to sit home and complain about what's wrong with AA.

Johnny L., October 1994

Honesty Is Our Ally
From Augusta, Georgia:

ALCOHOL ADDICTS, drug addicts, or dually-addicted persons who, for whatever reason, do not have the capacity to be honest about themselves will drop out of AA eventually, and ultimately I will have benefited from knowing and sharing recovery experiences with them.

My desire is for everyone to experience the power of the AA program, but I have learned from painful experience that I don't have control over the selection process. I have listened to, heard, and accepted the words of wisdom from AA members who have achieved sobriety through the Twelve Steps, and that wisdom is: 1) I should carry the message of recovery; and 2) I can't give away what I ain't got.

D.H., September 1986

A Mania for Alcohol
From Del City, Oklahoma:

I'VE BEEN A SOBER member of AA for seven years. My drinking career was brief, spanning only seven years. But when I came into AA at twenty-one, I was already a chronic rumhound.

Like many younger members of AA, I used substances other than alcohol during my drinking career. However, alcohol was what dominated my life. The chapter on Step Six in the "Twelve and Twelve" talks about the "mania for alcohol" in our lives (page 64). That description fits me perfectly. I had a mania for alcohol.

I was arrested for drinking and driving three times—not for smoking, shooting, or popping pills and driving. My ego and my craving for alcohol were at the center of my life.

I remember hearing a friend in AA telling me a truth about alcoholics. He said that in order for a person to become an alcoholic that person must consume alcohol. I became an alcoholic because I drank alcohol to excess—not because I drank milk or tea to excess or because I smoked or swallowed drugs.

AA's singleness of purpose is important to me because it constantly reminds me that AA exists to bring the message of recovery from alcoholism to alcoholics. Because our alcoholism is the only malady that we all have in common, our singleness of purpose reminds us that we are to stay sober and help other alcoholics to achieve sobriety.

Because AA existed and carried the message of sobriety and serenity to me seven years ago, and because of the love of one drunk for another drunk, I am filled with gratitude.

James M., October 1994

It Has To Begin with Me
From Corpus Christi, Texas:

I RECENTLY CELEBRATED my thirty-second birthday; I have nine years' sobriety. At most AA meetings I've attended in the United States, Canada, and the Far East, the AA Preamble has been read at the beginning of each meeting. I don't believe the basic purpose of AA could be put in simpler nor more understandable terms: "Our primary purpose is to stay sober and help other alcoholics to achieve sobriety."

But I can't stay sober on only one hour per day, nor can I carry any type of message and help others on just one hour per day. I was taught to learn how to live sober outside AA meetings, by spending time with AA members outside AA meetings. As I understand my sobriety, a loving God has given my life back one day at a time, and that will continue, provided I follow directions. If I want those who come into AA to have what I had when I came in, then it has to begin with me. I don't live my life only in AA meetings and I don't practice these principles only when I get to the door of the clubhouse where the group meets.

AA is not a self-help program, a therapy group, nor an extension of a treatment center. It is a program of Twelve Steps in which we experience a psychic change or spiritual experience after working the Steps. This is what I want new members to have when they walk in the door of my home group.

Mike F., October 1994

Around the Tables
From Houston, Texas:

I CAME INTO AA when I was fifteen years old. Until then, I had no purpose in life. I didn't want to go on like I was, but I was afraid to try something different. At first I couldn't understand anything about the Steps, Traditions, or Big Book except the phrase I heard at meetings: "Keep coming back, it works." I knew I had to keep coming back; otherwise I would have died out there. I went back out twice at the start of the recovery process; today I have over seven years, one day at a time.

I heard my future told around the tables at my home group if I kept going like I was, and I also heard what my future could be if I got sober and stayed that way. My singleness of purpose today is to stay sober and help other alcoholics to achieve sobriety.

Allen D., October 1994

Keeping It Simple
From Lincoln, Nebraska:

AFTER GOING TO MEETINGS for thirty days, I took my last drink on August 5, 1988. I was twenty-two years old. Although I didn't realize it until now, AA's singleness of purpose has meant a lot to me.

When I showed up at your doors, you kept it very simple for me. You said, "Don't drink, go to meetings, get a sponsor, and keep coming back." You said that if I did this, things would get better. You didn't tell me *when* but I believed you just the same. There was no evaluation process, no fees to pay, no people I needed to see, or appointments that I needed to make. I just showed up at the meetings and you loved me. I was an alcoholic who wanted a new way of life, and that was all you cared about. I believe it's the simplicity of AA, based on our singleness of purpose, that makes AA not only easily accessible to every alcoholic but creates a program that really works.

From conversations I've had with people who have come to AA via treatment centers, I can understand why our singleness of purpose is getting lost. Treatment centers do not have a singleness of purpose or the Traditions; their clients are counseled on everything from drugs and alcohol to co-dependency, child abuse, incest, anger control, dysfunctional families — the list goes on and on. It's no wonder that by the time these people get to AA, they see themselves as "alcoholic and a . . . ." It also follows that when in an AA meeting, many people continue to discuss all these issues.

I don't believe that this is a real threat to AA. Most of the people I see who maintain this mentality that "I'm addicted to everything" usually don't stick around too long. I for one don't blame them. If you had told me in the beginning what I was going to have to do, I never would have come back.

I was at a meeting one night when a man got his five-year chip and said, "I didn't come into Alcoholics Anonymous to get a beautiful wife, a nice home, and a new car; to be blessed with two wonderful children, or a host of new friends. I came to AA to get sober, and in staying sober I received all that and so much more." This to me really sums up what I'm trying to say. If I stay focused on sobriety and my disease of alcoholism, the multitude of other problems I have will eventually work their way to the surface. Then with the tools I have available in AA, they can be dealt with, one at a time.

One last thing. I think it's wonderful when people find the courage to seek help outside AA when necessary. But I believe it's a mistake to bring these things into an AA meeting. A newer member or somebody not listening closely may interpret what you say as a part of our recovery program when really it isn't. This only serves to dilute the AA message and maybe lead someone from our proven Twelve Steps.

My sobriety, and the sobriety of those to come, depends on the simplicity of AA and on our singleness of purpose.

Terry R., October 1994

Opinions Anonymous?
From Bellevue, Nebraska:

I'M YOUNG IN SOBRIETY and not exactly old in age, and I would like to describe a recent event that happened to me. One of the opportunities for AA service work in my area is taking a meeting into a women's detention center. One week, as usual, one of the women volunteered to read the Steps out loud before the meeting. In the process, she added the words "or her" wherever God was referred to as "him." This bothered me but I didn't say anything at the time.

The following week I asked that the Steps be read as they were written, without any added words. All went fine until one of the women asked why I'd made the request. I tried to explain that everyone in AA is perfectly free to have her own concept of God, but by adding words to the Steps a person could easily get the idea that we were trying to define God.

Of course, each woman had her own opinion on this and some shared it. Before I knew it, our AA meeting had turned into a wide-ranging discussion about different concepts of God. Then the woman who had brought the meeting in with me said we were all there for an AA meeting; if anyone was interested they could continue to discuss these ideas after the meeting.

This is a perfect example that our primary purpose must remain alcoholism. This is what binds us together.

Cheryl A., October 1994

Cooperation Not Affiliation
From Poughkeepsie, New York:

I SEE PEOPLE struggling at AA meetings with the concept of keeping the focus of their discussion on alcohol. I want to share my own experience in the hope that others may learn from my mistakes. My first sponsor was addicted to cocaine and had not abused alcohol in over ten years when he came into AA. I felt comfortable with him because I was also addicted to cocaine and didn't think that I'd abused alcohol as seriously as I had other drugs.

Many other newcomers in my area also seemed to be like my sponsor and me, with problems other than alcohol that needed to be addressed. But when we started to share in meetings about our drug histories, we were told to keep the focus on alcohol.

A counselor from the alcohol treatment center I'd been to was very helpful to me. She suggested I might feel more comfortable at Narcotics Anonymous (NA) meetings. I took her suggestion and began to attend NA meetings on a regular basis. In NA I learned that I suffer from the disease of addiction and must abstain from all drugs in order to recover.

As the months passed, however, I began to slack up on NA meetings. There wasn't as much variety in meetings in my hometown as I would have liked and I didn't have the willingness to humble myself and ask people for rides to meetings out of town. I was setting myself up for a relapse.

Finally I reached out for help. A friend suggested that I start attending AA meetings again on a regular basis. After reaching an emotional and spiritual bottom, that's exactly what I did.

As my first year of sobriety passed, I was attending an average of seven AA meetings and three NA meetings per week, and maintaining an active service commitment in both Fellowships. I was told by people in NA that I didn't need AA, and people in AA told me I didn't need NA for my addictions to other substances. I felt torn and resentful to hear people on both sides trashing the other Fellowship. After a couple of years of this, I finally found a new sponsor in AA and cut down on my NA meetings to one or two a month.

This new sponsor helped me see things in a whole new light. I began to see how important it is to separate my addiction to alcohol from my addictions to other substances. It was vital for me to focus totally on my drinking in order to shed light on any minimizing that I might be doing and to root out other forms of denial. My initial surrender had been due to my powerlessness over drugs, but deep in the back of my mind I was still romancing a drink. AA's singleness of purpose helped me to finally hear my own story.

The relationship between the AA Fellowship and the NA Fellowship should be one of cooperation not affiliation. I believe the public information committees of both Fellowships can work together to help newcomers find a consistent message of hope and ongoing recovery in either Fellowship.

NA needs the support of the many dual addicts who are in recovery in AA. As for myself, I shall continue to support both Fellowships in gratitude. As I look back on all the problems I've had trying to juggle the two, I see that most of my troubles were the result of misinformation.

Let's take the path of wisdom and use our past troubles as lessons to grow by.

K.B., June 1999

Chapter 6

❖

YOUR MOVE: SEPTEMBER 1999

The Lord's Prayer at AA Meetings

*I*n this chapter, letters were written in response to the topic of two February 1999 articles: "A Contradiction in Terms" and "How Others See Us" addressed the question of the appropriateness of saying the Lord's Prayer at AA meetings. Both writers thought that the prayer was distinctly sectarian and violated the Traditions. One writer said that "for more than half the world's population, this 'universal' prayer poses serious problems." Following the articles, the Grapevine printed a 1959 letter from Bill W., who wrote that "it is sometimes complained that the Lord's Prayer is a Christian document." He went on to write that "it seems only right that at least the Serenity Prayer and the Lord's Prayer be used in connection with our meetings. It does not seem necessary to defer to the feelings of our agnostic and atheist newcomers to the extent of completely hiding our light under a bushel."

❖

Avoiding Dubious Luxuries
From Crosby, Minnesota:

I'M A CHRISTIAN and I join in prayerfully when everyone holds hands and says the "Our Father"—at mass every Sunday. Personally, I think church is where it should stay. Using the Lord's Prayer at AA meetings clearly violates several Traditions, especially the Third and Fourth. Bill W. writes about the Third Tradition: "Why did we dare say, contrary to the experience of society and government everywhere, that we must never compel anyone to pay anything, believe anything, or conform to anything?" I thought for a long time that Tradition Four actually supported the use of the prayer, by granting autonomy to each group, but I have come to believe that its usage can negatively affect Alcoholics Anonymous as a whole. When I am privileged to chair our Tuesday night meeting, I pass out copies of the Seventh Step prayer to close with.

Having said this, I also know that anger and resentment are the dubious luxuries of normal people. So when others choose to close with the Lord's Prayer, I happily join in, keeping an eye out for anyone who may seem uncomfortable, which provides me another opportunity to share my experience, strength, and hope.

Doug P.

Remember Our Primary Purpose
From Amarillo, Texas:

OUR PREAMBLE SAYS "AA is not allied with any politics, sect, denomination, organization, or institution." I believe AA has done an admirable job of this generally, although I know of groups that appear to have been assimilated by the churches in which their meetings are held.

There are two points to remember: First, AA evolved from the Oxford Group, which was a Christian organization. Both Bill W. and Dr. Bob had been associated with these groups, and adapted their format and precepts to form an organization to help alcoholics achieve and maintain sobriety.

Second, although it was the intent of the founders to create a nonsectarian, nonreligious spiritual organization, U.S. society in the nineteen-thirties, forties, and fifties was less diverse than it is today. The first members adopted a prayer by a Christian theologian to become the well-loved Serenity Prayer. The Lord's Prayer was viewed as a benign inclusion because it was common to all Christian denominations.

Since then, due to the need for an effective way to combat alcoholism everywhere, AA has grown to include many more members of the Jewish faith as well as Buddhists, Hindus, Moslems, Native Americans, and people of other belief systems. Most embrace the concept of a Higher Power. Atheists and agnostics, upon coming into AA, also find the need for a Higher Power, even though it be the group itself, to rely on to achieve sobriety.

There is nothing I know of in AA Traditions to prevent those who are uncomfortable with the prayers their group uses from holding a group conscience meeting and adopting other prayers. Nor is there anything to prevent such persons from forming a home group where they feel free to pray to their Higher Power in their own way. Every faith has a richness of prayers that could be adapted to an AA group.

Let us not allow religious differences within AA to become a source of resentment and divert us from our primary purpose: "to stay sober and help other alcoholics to achieve sobriety."

Kay H.

An Expression of Gratitude
From Merritt Island, Florida:

WHY CLOSE A MEETING with a prayer? Because many of us believe that meetings should be spiritual. We like to thank our Higher Power for the new life, the second chance, he has given us.

The Lord's Prayer was developed by a dissident named Jesus, who was crucified for his radical teachings. He gave the prayer to a bunch of folks sitting on a hillside who had asked, "How should we pray?" In our Great American Experiment, "One Nation Under God," most of us have adopted the prayer simply because it does well what it was intended to do.

Anonymous

Tradition Trashing?
From San Luis Obispo, California:

FIRST, I'D LIKE TO STATE that I believe the Lord's Prayer to be such an expression of "good living" that it may well be a standard by which other prayers might be judged—and, often, found lacking. However, I must salute the author of "A Contradiction in Terms?" for her well-constructed argument concerning the ritual recitation of this prayer within the supposed nonsectarian confines of Alcoholics Anonymous.

I have long been concerned with this practice, and I quickly dismiss the rebuttal that "it's been this way forever!" That argument carries the same amount of weight as it does when applied to another Tradition-trashing practice like men's stag or women's closed meetings. Sure, these practices have been with AA since Bill and Bob. That doesn't make them right. And Bill W.'s comments following this article come as no surprise either; they sound suspiciously like the rebuffs I hear from some members today—altogether unconvincing and leaning toward the "if God chases 'em out, booze'll chase 'em back in" camp. This view ignores five of our Twelve Traditions.

Early on I heard that, because of the Traditions, AA was virtually invincible from outside forces, but if it were to crumble, it would be "an inside job."

God—Jesus, Allah, Buddha, Brahma, K'ungfutze, the Tao, Ahura Mazda, Whatever—save us from ourselves.

Erik R.

When in Rome
From Korea:

I GOT SOBER in August 1993, and the spiritual angle of the AA program came hard to me. I was a diehard atheist, and when I first saw the word "God" at an AA meeting, I was almost out of my seat. At that time, I had a strong resentment against the religion of my childhood.

Fortunately, no one in AA pressured me to choose a particular conception of God; if they had, I would have chosen death by alcoholism instead. I simply couldn't accept a life based on spiritual principles through the medium of religion, but through AA's Twelve Steps I could. I worked the Steps as best I could, and by the time I got to Step Twelve, I was no longer an atheist; I'd acquired a faith in a power greater than myself (though I'm still not a member of a religious body). The words "as we understand Him" allowed me to stay in Alcoholics Anonymous; they saved my life.

The article "A Contradiction in Terms?" seems to argue that AA meetings are not accommodating enough to members like me. I have at times shared the concerns expressed by the author. However, upon careful self-examination (using Step Ten), I came to realize that my fears were centered on an unreasonable resentment: No one likes to be in the out-group, the minority—not in school, society, or AA. Many of us drank in order to feel a part of the crowd.

So it's important that we non-Christians can share our stories with the newcomer and make it clear that a Christian faith is not a prerequisite to continuous sobriety. We can be vocal without being evangelical. If the newcomer is truly interested in our solution, he will hear us loud and clear.

I've been active in AA in the Midwest and Southwest, and also spent a year in France attending French-speaking meetings. Each region has its dominant culture, and the people inhabiting these regions have necessarily brought their culture and their religion to the AA meetings. Religious differences as well as cultural differences—including race, the effects of economic prosperity or depression, small town life vs. life in the big city—were everywhere apparent in the personalities at the meetings, but not in the principles.

I'm not going to influence the prevailing culture—not in America, not in Europe, and not here in East Asia. So, when in Rome, I do as the Romans do. I have found it best to adhere to the principles of AA without developing resentments against some of its personalities.

The principles of AA do not belong to the American, white, educated, middle-class, primarily male culture that its founders belonged to, nor are the principles exclusively Christian. But AA developed here in America; let us not begrudge the fact that this country is predominantly Christian.

I have always felt free to be myself in AA—for the first time in my life. Let us nonChristians and Christians alike be examples of acceptance and understanding. AA needs us all.

I must not finish sharing on this topic without expressing my deep thanks to AA's many religious members for the great job they do of keeping their religion separate from AA.

Anonymous

In the Circle
From Raytown, Missouri:

MY HOME GROUP ends each meeting with "May we close in the usual manner for all who care to join?" At this point, I can hold hands, pray aloud, or pray whatever comes to me silently. Or I can leave the meeting. For me, this moment is a spot-check inventory—a matter for the conscience of the individual member. I feel the spiritual energy and beauty that sings around our hand-linked circle of recovery. It is the effort that matters. This is merely an opportunity to improve my conscious contact with the God of my understanding.

"Love and tolerance of others is our code." Tradition Two is always ready for use.

Quinn G.

No Doubt
From Saint John, New Brunswick:

IN HIS LAST TALK, Dr. Bob stated clearly that the answer to our problem was in the Good Book, the Bible. The absolute essentials were the Sermon on the Mount, which includes the Our Father or Lord's Prayer, the thirteenth chapter of First Corinthians, and the Book of James.

So why is using the Lord's Prayer at AA meetings being challenged? I'd prefer not to doubt the success of Dr. Bob and Bill W.

Ivan M.

Invitation to Discussion
From Hampton, New Jersey:

I DO NOT PARTICIPATE in the pernicious chanting at the close of meetings, and it gives me a resentment, but I do participate in the Lord's Prayer. As with other alcoholics, I've always had a problem with alienation—feeling different, special, superior, inferior—and encountering the Lord's Prayer at my first few meetings certainly reinforced my feelings of alienation. I refused to recite it. I remained respectfully silent but felt apart and different.

At an earlier stage of my disease, I might have bolted out of the room and I might well be dead today instead of ten years sober. But I quickly realized that my feelings of resistance to the Lord's Prayer could easily be extended to other aspects of the AA program that I couldn't understand, or to individuals' ideas and personalities I didn't like. I knew I had a problem with intolerance, and this might be a threat to my hopes of getting sober and finding spirituality.

So I decided to participate in the Lord's Prayer, although it has no meaning for me. I notice others in the room remaining silent, with expressions of discomfort on their faces. I know how they feel.

Anonymous

A Brief Comment
No location given:

THERE ARE MANY WORDS I could use to describe using the Lord's Prayer in AA meetings, but the kindest is "insensitive."

Anonymous

Prayer of the Heart
From Aloha, Oregon:

WHEN I CAME to Alcoholics Anonymous, I didn't think that the Lord's Prayer could possibly work for me, but I also knew that my own perceptions of what would or wouldn't work were all screwed up. I was in no state to figure out what parts of AA were necessary and what weren't, so I did everything. Surrendering to the wisdom of people who were managing to stay sober was essential. I was told that if I wanted what you had, I had to do what you did, and that seemed to include the Lord's Prayer.

The longer I stayed sober, the more my faith in a Higher Power of my own understanding grew and evolved. By the time I'd been sober for six or seven years, this faith had developed into something very different from the theology expressed in the Lord's Prayer. I started changing a word here and a word there in that prayer so I could say it and still be true to my own belief. I reached a point where I was doing so much rewriting it seemed silly, so I let my mouth say the Lord's Prayer on autopilot (my mouth goes on autopilot rather easily!) while I mentally prayed the prayer that was in my heart.

This worked fine for several years. Then, about a year ago, that method of praying began to feel like another layer of the onion ready to be peeled away. I stopped saying the Lord's Prayer, and now I say my heart's prayer, quietly, so as not to distract the people around me.

It amazes me that this is so easy and so comfortable. I can still participate fully in the Fellowship and can let "all that is within me bless God's holy name" together with the rest of my AA family, without having to say a prayer that isn't true to my own beliefs or experience.

Occasionally someone will tell me to "keep comin' back," that I'll get the spiritual part of the program if I just stick around long enough. Such folks challenge me to practice patience, tolerance, and the biting of my tongue. I can also pray (silently!) that they will stick around long enough to understand the principles of AA.

The Big Book says, "We found the Great Reality deep down within us. In the last analysis it is only there that it may be found." And I know the importance of the idea "To your own self be true."

Karen O.

A Policy of Attraction?
From Roswell, Georgia:

I RECENTLY READ that in New York, a federal appellate court has upheld a ruling that an atheist cannot be forced by the court to attend AA. The man, convicted of a charge of driving while intoxicated, was ordered to attend AA meetings but sued on the grounds of religious freedom because "meetings involve religious exercises." The court agreed that "the religious nature of the meetings" would violate his rights as an atheist. The U.S. Court of Appeals upheld the ruling.

While we insist that we are not a religious organization, it seems that we are the only ones who perceive ourselves so. The perception of the general public, and now the courts, is that we are a religious organization. How will this affect our policy of "attraction"?

Donna F.

The Delicate Thread
From Tucson, Arizona:

MY HOME GROUP recently undertook the debate about changing our closing format to include something other than the Lord's Prayer. It has been my experience that when an attempt to understand the full significance of the Lord's Prayer in an AA meeting is made, one of two things occurs: either a debate ensues over principles, or an argument takes place between personalities. Debate can be a rigorous discussion how to best apply those principles, guided by the Traditions of AA; the argument occurs when a group member feels that her or his personal beliefs are being attacked. In my experience, too many AAs get stuck in the personal rather than in the principle.

In a 1961 Grapevine article (reprinted in *The Language of the Heart*), Bill W. states, "The phrase 'God as we understand him' is perhaps the most important expression to be found in our whole AA vocabulary. Within the compass of these five significant words there can be included every kind and degree of faith, together with the positive assurance that each of us may choose his own."

I believe that making an invitation to pray to a Higher Power using a Judeo-Christian prayer, with no alternative except to stand in silent compliance, is clearly coercive. The implementation of a defined Higher Power in prayer ("Our Father who art in heaven") eliminates personal choice to the individual AA member, and continued use of this prayer implies affiliation with something that is not AA. The message that is subtly being delivered is: "Here we pray to a God of our understanding—and you are expected to do the same."

In that same article, Bill W. goes on to say, "In AA's first years I all but ruined the whole undertaking with this sort of unconscious arrogance. God as *I* understood him *had* to be for everybody. Sometimes my aggression was subtle and sometimes it was crude. But either way it was damaging—perhaps fatally so—to numbers of nonbelievers." Spiritual pride, as Bill W. coined the term, can be fatal.

I hear a lot of spiritual pride when my fellow AAs come to the defense of the Lord's Prayer. It sometimes borders on spiritual arrogance. Bill W. asks us to ask ourselves if "we are not more subject to fits of spiritual pride than we had supposed. If constantly worked at, I'm sure that no kind of self-survey could be more beneficial. Nothing could more surely increase our communication with each other and with God." This spiritual pride can also be fatal to the group because it decreases communication by emphasizing the differences between us instead of finding a common ground.

Tradition Five states that each group has but one primary purpose—to carry its message to the alcoholic who still suffers. But we skate on thin ice every time someone driven by spiritual pride chooses to defend the use of the Lord's Prayer because of how it personally affects him or her. How many suffering alcoholics have been spooked away because of the prayer? How long will it take before we begin to look at whether we are, in fact, carrying the message? One alcoholic who turns away is one too many.

Finally, Tradition Ten guides us away from any controversy which can divert us from our primary purpose. Every one of us has a personal opinion about politics, religion, and even alcohol itself. As the early AAs went through their own squabbles over personal opinion, they learned a valuable lesson that they passed on to us: "Since recovery from alcoholism is life itself to us, it is imperative that we preserve in full strength our means of survival" (*Twelve Steps and Twelve Traditions*). There are too many breaks with the Traditions revolving around the Lord's Prayer to simply dismiss the controversy with

"It's the way it's always been done" or "If it ain't broke, don't fix it."

When discussing the appropriateness of using the Lord's Prayer in AA, let us remember the delicate thread that binds us and is maintained through principles rather than personalities. We are, after all, simply messengers. Let us try not to lose sight of what that message is.

Claudia R.

Keep on Rockin'
From Hightstown, New Jersey:

I'M ALWAYS GLAD to get the Grapevine in the mail—I'm even grateful for the articles that get me upset because then I find something in myself that needs work. The February issue was a case in point. Being a Christian, I immediately took offense at someone not wanting to say the Lord's Prayer. This is what I got sober with, and it meant a lot to me to hear it at the end of a meeting. But after much thought, I came to some conclusions.

On one hand, saying the Lord's Prayer might turn some new people off. I can understand this feeling because I was once at a meeting on a Native American reservation, and the meeting ended with a prayer to the Great Spirit. I felt a bit uncomfortable, not because they were saying a different prayer, but because I didn't understand what it meant to them. After talking with the elders, my perspective changed. What I found out was that the prayer was not for me but for those who need it. I can enjoy the fact that God (or whatever you want to call it) works in many wonderful ways.

On the other hand, I love the fact that the Traditions give our groups the chance to decide for themselves how they want to end a meeting. If ninety percent of the meeting is Buddhist, there will probably be a Buddhist prayer at the end, and that is wonderful—I for one would enjoy it.

Freedom and change are the keys to me. Allowing everyone to believe in what they need to believe is important; I hope we'll all remember to listen to the minority voice. This is what I was taught by my sponsors, who believed that everyone's opinion matters.

That's why I love the topics the Grapevine throws out. Don't be afraid to rock the boat—we need it!

Darek H.

Chapter 7

❖

THE PRACTICE OF ANONYMITY

Ensuring "Great Blessings"

*B*ill W.'s conviction that AA needed some guiding
principles, or Traditions, to ensure its future survival,
were set forth in a series of articles published in the magazine
from 1946 through 1948. In "A Tradition Born of Anonymity"
(January 1946, reprinted in *The Language of the Heart*), Bill
wrote that while anonymity was of value to AA's public
relations policy, its greatest importance might be personal:
". . . we are beginning to feel that the word 'anonymous' has
for us an immense spiritual significance. Subtly but
powerfully it reminds us that we are always to place
principles before personalities; that we have renounced
personal glorification in public; that our movement not only
preaches, but actually practices a truly humble
modesty." In this chapter, AAs describe how they
have grappled with questions of
anonymity: At what level should it be
observed? What does it mean to
individual AA members? How does it
help us in the practical matter of
staying sober?

❖

No Experts in AA
From Wilmington, North Carolina:

IN OUR FAIRLY SMALL TOWN, just about everybody knows everybody else. That is especially true in the AA community—I know who is an attorney, a doctor, a printer, or an employee at the local treatment center.

When I confer with professionals—who happen to be AAs—at their places of business, they offer me recommendations and analyses based on their expertise; I go to them because I respect their professional judgment. However, when I run into these professionals at AA meetings, I must be careful to treat them as I do other recovering alcoholics. What they have to share with me at meetings is what any other member has: their own experience, strength, and hope; what they have learned about their illness; how they practice the AA program in their own lives. They're no different from the rest of us—we're all imperfect human beings, trying to grow in sobriety. I need to allow a professional to be just another AA member; they must have the chance to use our beautiful program to work on their own recovery, to share the good and the bad in their daily lives.

By the same token, the professionals can learn to leave their professionalism outside the meeting doors. Maybe I can help them do that: I can avoid asking for advice, and I can even stop the advice-givers and lecturers in meetings (in a very loving way, of course).

Thank God, there are no experts in AA. We are all one drink away from a drunk, no matter what length or quality of sobriety we have, or what we do for a living.

S.G., September 1985

Misconception
From Binghamton, New York:

THE PREVALENT MISCONCEPTION about what anonymity is supposed to embrace is sometimes cause for hurt feelings. For example, to use a fellow member's last name, and to have guilt about this, is indeed silly.

What is meant in the writings on anonymity by those who founded AA was in regard to the unmanageable ego that erupted when exposed to press, radio, and films. The hideous and huge "I, I, I" so detrimental to us all, accompanied by vain ambition, was meant to be opposed by the doctrine of anonymity. Knowing last names has nothing whatever to do with it.

A.K., December 1981

Anonymity on the Job
From Vancouver, British Columbia:

THE PRINCIPLE OF ANONYMITY carries great blessings when applied to an individual's life. The Twelfth Tradition says this about anonymity: "It reminds us that we are to place principles before personalities; that we are actually to practice a genuine humility. This to the end that our great blessings may never spoil us . . . ."

Here is another consideration. I find that when I remain anonymous, I feel more confident in expressing my innermost feelings and memories to other recovering alcoholics. I can leave my workday identity, and facades, behind. While the social stigma of being a "known alcoholic" may have lessened these past years, it is still around.

Let me give an example from my own life. My workplace is a pleasant public service area, teeming with people. My supervisor is a seasoned, understanding woman, well liked by everyone—a "people person."

One of my coworkers is, like me, a recovering alcoholic. We first met at an AA meeting—he had recently been released from an institution and was doing a remarkable job of recovery. We'll call him Mr. A. One day at work, Mr. A. decided to talk about the AA program to me while our supervisor was within earshot. Inadvertently or otherwise, Mr. A. broke our anonymity. He mentioned my going to meetings and also started to talk about other people we know from the Fellowship. I asked Mr. A. to refrain from this conversation, but not before our supervisor had overheard us.

I remember very well how she gave me an embarrassed look, as though she felt she'd heard something inappropriate, not meant for her ears. Mr. A. was oblivious to all this, but I felt humiliated. I didn't know how my supervisor might react.

As it turned out my supervisor made only one reference to my recovery from alcoholism. A few months later she approached me with her concerns about another employee, whom I'll call Mr. B. She said she felt Mr. B. might have a drinking problem and wondered if I would talk to him about AA.

This story has a positive ending, thanks to my Higher Power, though it could just as easily have been otherwise. I did acquaint Mr. B. with the AA program, and while I don't see him often, it seems his quality of life has been improving. As for Mr. A., he went on to another job more in his field, and I haven't seen him for a while. I hope he has learned to respect our principle of anonymity.

My supervisor and I continue to have a good relationship—I feel fortunate that she had an open mind about our Fellowship, in view of the fact that she knew very little about it. As for me? I'm enjoying my seventh year of anonymous sobriety, in thankful contemplation.

J.M., September 1989

The Anonymity of Others
From Arcadia, California:

I'D LIKE TO SHARE a recent experience. I had a work assignment in a small, isolated community in northern Arizona, and found that the contact phone numbers in the AA World Directory were hopelessly out of date. I tried a number listed in the directory for another town in Arizona, and the individual I reached also had the out-of-date phone numbers. Okay, so now what?

As it happened, I had a minor medical problem and had to see a local doctor. I asked him if he knew any local AA members. Not surprisingly (the local medical community often knows at least one member of AA), he offered several numbers.

I am thankful that the AAs of that community hadn't been hiding in total anonymity, or I never would have made contact with some very fine people. I was welcomed immediately once I made contact.

This incident points up to me that to have attraction, we have to be known to others beyond ourselves.

W.G., December 1974

How Anonymous To Be?
From Oakridge, Oregon:

ON PAGE 264 of *Dr. Bob and the Good Oldtimers*, Dr. Bob is quoted as having said that "there were two ways to break the anonymity Tradition: 1) by giving your name at the public level of press or radio; 2) by being so anonymous that you can't be reached by other drunks."

The book then quoted the Grapevine, in an article dated February 1969, where Dr. Bob allegedly commented on the anonymity Tradition as follows: "Since our Tradition on anonymity designates the exact level where the line should be held, it must be obvious to everyone who can read and understand the English language that to maintain anonymity at any other level is definitely a violation of this Tradition.

"The AA who hides his identity from his fellow AA by using only a given name violates the Tradition just as much as the AA who permits his name to appear in the press in connection with matters pertaining to AA."

Ernie G. (another old-timer involved in the beginnings of AA) also commented, "We don't know anyone's last name. They get so doggone carried away with this anonymity that it gets to be a joke. I had a book [evidently a small address book compiled by early members or their wives] with the first hundred names—first and last—telephone numbers, and where they lived."

Further, Dr. Bob felt that it was important to let yourself be known in the community as an AA member. So evidently the Tradition for anonymity was designed mainly to protect the newcomer in his or her newfound sobriety, to enable us to get a new start in life while becoming established in the Fellowship.

In my opinion, we would do better to worry less about whether we scare off newcomers by using the word *God* or about the dual-addiction question, and concentrate on the bonding of unity in our Fellowship. We need to know who we are and how to contact one another.

J.A., September 1989

The Robe of Anonymity?
From Bowling Green, Ohio:

CAN WE RETAIN our anonymity? In my opinion, that is a question of circumstance.

Our group is located in a small city in the northwestern part of our state, and Alcoholics Anonymous has become almost an institution here. It is a small group but a growing one, and our growth can be credited in part to the cooperation which we receive from the clergy and officers of the law.

These good people feel free to call upon any member of the group at any time, and tell of someone who needs help. To these folks, AA is a clearinghouse for any drunk who desires aid. Should we clothe ourselves in a robe of anonymity? It seems to me that, in this case, it would defeat the purpose of AA indefinitely.

Don't think that we broadcast the fact that we belong to AA. In our community that has been unnecessary. Most of us were very conspicuous in our drinking days, and when we had accepted AA and tried to live the Twelve Steps, that also made us conspicuous in the eyes of the law and the citizens of our town.

We never were ashamed of our escapades when we were drinking; should we be ashamed when we have become rehabilitated and are living decent, respectable lives?

D.M., June 1950

It's Not Who You Know
From Columbus, Ohio:

WHEN I ASKED a man if he would be my sponsor, he said, "Yes, I will, but you need to know that I have done some illegal things in sobriety."

A month later I was talking to my brother, trying to impress him with my newfound sobriety, and I told him who I'd asked to be my sponsor. His mouth dropped open and he said, "Are you aware I'm suing that __ of a ___?"

First I had to go to my sponsor and confess how I had broken his anonymity. When I searched myself for the reasons I had done this, I found that my self-worth was involved. I'd always believed that my place in life depended on whom I knew, and who knew that I knew whom I knew. That certainly was true when I joined a fraternity in college, and over the years this trait had become more insidious.

But AA's concept of anonymity destroyed my most treasured tool for social enhancement. All of a sudden I wasn't allowed to tell people who my friends were. I didn't even know their last names.

I'm so grateful for the principle of anonymity. It was this concept that broke through my dependence on other people for my self-esteem. The Twelfth Tradition led me through the early days, and introduced me to the set of principles that set me free—the Twelve Steps.

As I sat in my brother's office that day, something inside me knew it was no coincidence that my sponsor was my sponsor. I intuitively knew that a power greater than myself had made the arrangement.

Anonymous, September 1989

True Blessings
From Palestine, Texas:

THE INDIVIDUAL WHO DOESN'T seem to care if the public knows he is a member of AA is taking on a double responsibility: to AA and to the groups around him. Suppose he slips: That will reflect on all AAs. The effect would not be too serious—but we all should want to add to AA and not detract.

There has been quite a lot of personal publicity of late in various groups here in Texas. I mean no personal criticism. Other people's opinions and consciences guide them as mine does me. But the founders of AA created a program that saved our lives, so we might do well to read and listen to their counsel, which says that the first, oldest, and most vital Tradition of AA is our anonymity. It proves that AA practices what it preaches, and that individual members are really giving of themselves and their experiences without thought of material return or personal publicity.

No one ever has to call attention to his own ability or virtue. His good qualities speak loudly for themselves. These qualities are not developed for the purpose of being talked about. They are to serve as a blessing to others. A true blessing is not a forced activity. It is a spontaneous act that goes out from the heart.

B., May 1948

No Photos, Please!
From Vancouver, British Columbia:

I'VE BEEN A GRATEFUL member of AA for nine months, and I have so much to learn. I am an avid reader of the Big Book and the Grapevine.

When I first came to AA, desperate and frightened, I was working in a business that was frequented by many members of the community, and I didn't want it to become public knowledge that I was in AA. So I was pleased to hear members saying that they protected other people's anonymity. And yet, on entering my third or fourth AA meeting, I saw that someone was "taking a cake"—an anniversary of four or five years of sobriety. This person had a friend with a camera who was indiscriminately taking photographs of the speakers and celebrants all through the meeting. None of us was asked for our consent, and most of the pictures were taken with the crowd in the background and the characteristic circle and triangle AA logo showing. When I was asked if I wanted to share during the meeting, I declined without explaining why, not wanting to spoil someone's "party." But was this not an AA meeting? It was listed in the directory as such. How many other newcomers were frightened at the prospect of photographs being taken and distributed who knows where?

If some members must take over a meeting with this show of pride, that is one thing. But if photographic memories are so important, why can't they wait until the meeting is closed, then draw their consenting friends aside and snap photos to their hearts' content?

As I grow in this program and through my Higher Power, I am more sensitive to the newcomers and the principles of AA. I now avoid any "cake" celebrations if I am forewarned. Am I the only person who feels this way? Have so many people forgotten what it was like to be newly sober? I pray I never do.

Anonymous, September 1989

Alone In Africa
No location given:

I'M THE WIFE of a U.S. ambassador overseas and a recovering alcoholic, so the principle of anonymity is of the utmost importance to me. In fact, it is so important that, rather than risk losing it by attending weekly AA meetings held in this African city, I have chosen to forgo attending meetings altogether.

This has not been as difficult as it seems since I have designed a very sound personal program based upon the principles I learned in a thirty-day stay at an East Coast rehab and the more than 200 meetings I attended before moving overseas. Additionally, I have a very supportive and wise husband who never hesitates to be my sounding board when I need to talk. I now have three years of sobriety.

The diplomatic life exposes me daily to situations where alcohol is served. I can firmly refuse offers of alcohol, thanks to a daily program of meditation, prayer, and AA reading, which has removed all desire to drink. It has become well-known to some stewards that my beverage of choice is always club soda with a wedge of lime, and I am often served this drink without even being asked.

So that I can satisfy the need to "give it away" in order to keep it, I have devoted hundreds of hours in fund-raising and volunteer work outside of AA to help the numerous disadvantaged and handicapped individuals who seem to overpopulate this Third World country where I live. I practice the AA principles in all my affairs, and if I can't be helping alcoholics, I am at least helping those who suffer from other diseases.

This is not a program which I recommend for anyone else, but it does work for me in my unique situation. When I am in the states on "R&R," I try to visit my home group and keep in touch with members by phone and letters. I read the Grapevine each month and have complete faith that God provides for me exactly what I need, one day at a time.

The situation has not occurred yet but if I thought that breaking my anonymity would help a suffering alcoholic toward recovery, I would do it in a minute.

Anonymous, September 1989

To the Newly Anonymous
From Alexandria, Virginia:

IF I HAD IT TO DO over, I'd keep it to myself I was an AA member, instead of enthusiastically telling everyone. Some people said, "For goodness' sake, I didn't know you drank like that!" Explanations were required. There was the friend who said, "Well, I wish you'd do something for that awful John Smith — look at his poor wife!" Explanations again: We cannot drag John Smith to a meeting without his consent. Then there was the neighbor who called: "There's a drunkard sitting on my doorstep. Please send an AA around!" More explanations: We are not the police. Her reply: "I thought it was your business to cure these drunkards!" Explanations: We can cure no one; only show him the way as shown to us. She said, "Well, it seems to me like you ought to do something to get this horrible man off my steps. I'd call my husband but he's at work." Explanations: We AAs also work. But if the man wishes contact with us, some AA members will gladly call after working hours. She got the last word anyhow: "I'm sorry I bothered you, but I thought you liked to help people!"

Another reason why I wish I'd kept my big mouth shut is because I tried answering questions after only two or three meetings, having only the vaguest conception of the real and magnificent purpose of AA and so no doubt gave incorrect replies and now wonder if I did not possibly do more harm than good.

But the most important reason why I wish I had held my silence is because of the words of Bill W. himself: "We . . . of Alcoholics Anonymous believe that the principle of anonymity has an immense spiritual significance."

C.D., December 1950

Inner Security
From Miller Place, New York:

SOME THOUGHTS ABOUT anonymity: It is leading me to a fully human life. The long form of the Twelfth Tradition describes the end to which the Steps are leading me. They put me in my place by setting forth a genuine humility—not a self-hating groveling, but rather an honest and loving relationship with a God who loves me. Once this is established, I am free to relate to other people out of the love and inner security that renders my overinflated ego superfluous.

J.T., September 1989

Anonymity and Me
No location given:

I'D BEEN SOBER four months and had kept my AA membership a dark secret. The inevitable day arrived when I received an invitation to my Uncle Paddy's home for one of our frequent—and liquid—family gatherings. Everyone greeted me with hoots of approval, telling me how marvelous I looked. All that evening I walked through the clan gathering while drinking soda. My hand trembled each time I poured a soft drink. After five hours, my Aunt Sarah looked at me and said, "I see you are drinking it in soda now, Ed." My family hadn't paid the least attention to what I had in my glass.

I made a decision to tell them my secret. They all agreed as how it was a grand thing, and they were all meaning to mention my drinking to me one of these days, and they knew AA was not full of bums anyway. The trauma of that evening could have been lessened for me if I'd understood that the anonymity Tradition applies at the public level and not the private. I grin now when I hear someone say that he broke his anonymity by telling his grandmother he was in AA.

We understand one another—anonymity and me.

E.S., February 1975

Principles Before Personalities
From Clearwater, Ontario:

WHEN I ATTENDED my first AA meeting four years ago, I was immediately attracted by the principle of anonymity. Despite the fact that my life had become unmanageable and I was in pain, there still remained a vestige of pride that kept me from wanting anyone to know who I was or what I did for a living. You see, I am an elementary school teacher.

Alcohol had beaten me down to a point where I was morally and emotionally bankrupt, and this didn't sit well with what I believed to be society's accepted ideal of a teacher of young children. I was acutely conscious of the fact that I was a creature beneath contempt.

But in AA, I could keep my identity a secret. It wasn't long, however, before my anonymity was threatened.

One night a couple of months after I'd been introduced to AA, a member of my home group approached me and declared, "I finally figured out who you are." I had taught her son a few years previously and she had just now recognized me. Initially, I was disturbed by this discovery, but after talking with her, I relaxed and soon forgot that I was her son's teacher and felt the friendship of one AA member for another.

As I attended a wider range of meeting places, I eventually met other members whose children I was presently teaching, and it became easier and easier to approach them, not in any professional capacity, but as a fellow AA.

Throughout this time I still carried with me one primary fear. Although I felt at ease talking with parents of my students within the Fellowship, I did have a fear of going to open AA meetings because I knew some of my pupils attended these meetings with their parents. I feared that my alcoholism would become a matter of public attention if ever I was seen at an open meeting. This then has been the motivation for me to attend mostly closed meetings in AA during the last few years.

Last December I was on call for the AA answering service when I received a Twelfth Step request from a man to take him to an AA meeting on the following night. Unfortunately for me, the meeting the next night was an open meeting, and I was faced with the old dilemma.

I told this caller I'd have to get back to him, and I pondered what to do. I was scared that my valued principle of anonymity would be threatened. Dare I take this man to an open meeting and risk seeing a student? Should I refer the newcomer to someone else for help?

The next night I picked up my new friend and went to the open meeting, feeling anxious about what would happen. I was not in the meeting more than ten minutes when I heard, "Hello, Mr. T." Turning around, I faced two of my students. Well, the sky didn't fall down, and they didn't ask me what I was doing there. We talked briefly and then parted as the meeting got started.

What these students of mine decide to do with their knowledge about me is beyond my control. Perhaps I don't give them enough credit for understanding AA principles even though they have parents actively involved in the program.

What I did learn from this entire episode was something about anonymity as it affects me.

Our Twelfth Tradition states: "Anonymity is the spiritual foundation of all our Traditions, ever reminding us to place principles before personalities." Prior to this open meeting, there was little of a spiritual nature in my understanding of anonymity. Certainly my personality had priority over the principle of service. It was that night when I began to see how anonymity as the spiritual foundation of my AA program is there not to protect me from you but to protect me from myself.

B.T., September 1989

Publicity Seekers
From Detroit, Michigan:

NOTWITHSTANDING BILL'S ARTICLE on anonymity [AA Grapevine, January 1946], which seemed to me to state the voice of experience pretty well on this crucial subject, there still seem to be a number of AAs who don't understand the reasons for anonymity.

My work calls for me to read newspapers and magazines from all over the country. At first I was astonished when I came on an article revealing the identity of some AA, with his or her obvious assistance. I'm no longer astonished—there have been too many cases—but I can't help worrying about it.

The reasons for anonymity seem plain to me. First, the promise of anonymity is certainly reassuring for the new prospect. Many would not come to AA if they thought their attendance was going to be made public. When they see the names of AA members splashed all around, they naturally doubt that we really mean we are anonymous and that they can be anonymous if they wish.

Second, anonymity prevents personal publicity exploits, those cases where an individual member cashes in personally by publicizing the fact that he or she is a member. In my opinion, this is pretty cheap stuff and certainly contrary to the spirit of AA. Anyone who uses AA to get publicity is scarcely honoring the AA concept of giving to others. This is plain, unvarnished seeking for personal gain.

Finally, the question is: What happens when one of these spotlight seekers falls flat on his or her face in full public view? What is the effect on AA then? Not good, certainly.

No one has any authority to set himself or herself up in public as being representative of AA in any respect. I don't want to be represented by these publicity seekers, and neither do a lot of other AAs.

The anonymity Traditions of AA are linked closely with the spiritual elements of our program: the humility, the giving without thought of return, the unselfish brotherhood, the noncommercialism and nonprofessionalism.

In short, anonymity is protection for the most important things — the priceless things — that we have in AA. Let's not let publicity seekers destroy them.

H.H., September 1947

The Thing in the Room
From Santa Barbara, California:

ABOUT ANONYMITY: When I came into AA twenty-five years ago, I expected members to be anonymous, because of the name of the organization. Thank God, they didn't force me to say my name or "state my disease" the way they do today. I was frightened and insecure, and very dependent on my husband who didn't want me to go to AA. We thought if people knew, his job might be adversely affected. Consequently, for the first five years in the Fellowship, I remained totally anonymous. I attended every meeting of my group. I diligently took the Steps as outlined, and I didn't pick up the first drink. I have stayed sober ever since, one day at a time.

Anonymity is the spiritual foundation of the program. It lets us know *what* is here while it keeps us from concentrating on *who* is here.

Sobriety is here. The newcomer can have it and it's free. When we are new, and we look into the eyes of the sober members in the room, we can see it working. It's been called "the thing in the room." It says that together we can stay sober. It says if I can do it, so can you.

I believe there are three ways to carry the message of sobriety: by example, by example, and by example. Talk is cheap. Forcing newcomers to talk sometimes puts their sick egos into full bloom, and minimizes their chances of sobriety. I got sober in a midwestern town where they didn't make newcomers talk. That was a godsend for me, because it permitted me to listen.

I am grateful that our founders had the foresight to call our Fellowship "Alcoholics Anonymous."

E.D., September 1989

Wise Spending
From Jackson Heights, New York:

ANONYMITY CAN BE LIKENED to one's money. How I spend my anonymity is my own business but I may not reach in another member's pocket or purse and spend his or her anonymity. Personally, I worry as little about my anonymity sober as I worried about my money drunk, but I certainly care more about the effects on how I spend my anonymity than I cared about what my money bought while drunk.

I hope I will always spend my anonymity wisely and with due thought for the good I may accomplish, rather than spend it with alcoholic grandiosity and egotism.

Phil W., August 1955

Carved in Stone
From Fátima, Portugal:

ON DR. BOB'S BURIAL STONE there is not a word about Alcoholics Anonymous. The co-founder of our Fellowship upheld the Twelfth Tradition to the grave. What an example of humility.

J.W., September 1989

Chapter 8

❖

YOUR MOVE: MARCH 1994

"Fine-Tuning" the Big Book

*G*raham M., an AA member in Canberra, Australia, wrote in September 1993 that after twenty-one years in AA, he was reexamining the language of the Big Book: "I can now see how many women . . . could feel excluded by the language of our basic text: Chapters two through eleven are mostly written in a way that assumes that both the reader and the recovering alcoholic described in the text are male." He went on to say that he didn't "think the text of the Big Book was divinely inspired and should never be altered . . . [or] is some kind of linguistic monument, chiselled in stone, never to be changed. It is an organic, growing, changing means of communication that, like a chisel itself, needs to be regularly sharpened to maintain its usefulness." The writer suggested that the Big Book be revised — or "fine-tuned" — in order to make it more effective in communicating to all alcoholics by forming a committee of women to offer appropriate revisions. The article stimulated a wide variety of responses.

❖

Taking Liberties
From London, Ontario:

TO BEGIN WITH, I've been a sober member of AA for thirty-seven years, and during this time I've met many other woman with the same length of sobriety, or longer, and, naturally, many with much less. I have met relatively few who felt wronged in any way by the manner in which the Big Book was written. Most of these women were grateful for the fact that the program of Alcoholics Anonymous offered them a practical solution to their problem; they weren't too concerned with whether their gender was spelled out or not.

It may be worth noting that in the era when the Big Book was written, in 1939, it was generally assumed that references to "man" or "mankind" included both male and female gender. I am also quite convinced after extensive study and reading of circumstances surrounding the writing of the Big Book that Bill and the others didn't write it with any intention of showing disregard for women or any other factor, such as color, creed, social or economic background.

The writer of the article says, "The Big Book is good, but not as effective as it could be." I'd like to point out that over the years, more and more people, including many outside of AA, both professionals and laymen, have written reports on the comprehensive manner in which the book was written and its effectiveness in providing a workable program for the benefit of alcoholics, as well as many with a variety of other human problems.

Can anyone imagine what would happen if a project were put forth to revamp and change the book to reflect personal preferences in regard to different facets of human nature?

Changing the personal stories section to reflect recovery experiences is one thing, but changing the original writings by Bill is another.

P.H.

Never Good Enough
From Clairton, Pennsylvania:

I WANT TO THANK Graham M. for his well-thought-out article. I'm sure I'm not alone when I say that as a woman, sober now fifteen years, I have struggled throughout my life with the misconception that I was somehow never quite good enough. Much of what we read or are told at work, at home, or in church seems to be aimed at the male gender exclusively, and that includes the Big Book. As a perfect example of Graham's point, page 29 reads: "Each individual, in the personal stories, describes in his own language and from his own point of view the way he established his relationship with God." How much more accurate the text would be if the "he/him" references were simply replaced with "they/their." Bill W. himself urged us, in every way possible, to be "inclusive rather than exclusive."

I realize that when the original text was written, there were few women members. Yet that has changed dramatically. Happily, of the forty-two stories now included at the back of the Big Book [the Third Edition], thirteen are about women.

Let the Big Book, in its entirety, continue to reach out to sick alcoholics, women and men alike.

J.P.

Making the Message Available
From Newport Beach, California:

"FINE-TUNING OUR BASIC TEXT" touched on a subject that myself and many other members have been talking about lately—the need for a more inclusive text in chapters two through eleven of the Big Book.

In fact, one of our women's meetings is a Big Book study meeting and when we read passages out loud from the book, we find it necessary to change "he" to "she." Although women alcoholics can relate to the experiences and the feelings talked about in the Big Book, the text can be confusing and make women alcoholics feel excluded.

I am a very grateful recovering woman alcoholic and I want to make sure the AA message is spread as effectively as possibly to all who need and want it.

S.F.

Revising History?
From Burbank, California:

THE WRITER OF THE ARTICLE states that "Alcoholics Anonymous should admit it has wronged women in the way the first third of the book is written." This is hard to justify, since the point of the book is only to show what the first hundred members understood to be the basics of their program. No attempt was made, and understandably so, to predict the unknown future and what role diversity might play in that future. There were several women in the original group, and the stories of two women appear in the First Edition.

From the vantage point of 1994, I think the first 164 pages should be viewed as a history book. They tell how a small group of people, during a narrow time period, evolved a program to get and stay sober. I was told early on: "Read the Big Book and find out how the first one hundred got sober. Then apply what you learn to yourself and build your own program accordingly."

The writer says that the Big Book is "an organic, growing, changing means of communication." God forbid! I have visions of George Orwell's novel *1984*, with its Ministry of Truth whose job was to constantly revise history to conform to the latest government policy. The Big Book was never intended to be an operating manual with revisions and constant updates, henceforth and forevermore.

If you want a politically correct, thoroughly modern, New Age operating manual, go ahead and write it.

Then see if it works.

D.B.

Individually Responsible
From Elk Grove, California:

I SEE THAT politically correct dogma is alive and well in at least one corner of the AA world scene. Well, why should revisionist history be limited to individuals, governments, and countries? Why not include the AA Fellowship and its Big Book in the action? Surely we can all benefit from this grand scheme to set straight the sins of omission and prejudice fostered by white European males and practiced in AA circles over the past fifty-eight years.

Of necessity, we will also be bound to examine Steps Three, Seven, and Eleven, along with Tradition Two. Political correctness demands that we eliminate words "him," "his," "he," and "himself." And since many, if not most, AA groups close their meetings with the Lord's Prayer, we have an attendant problem with the reference to "our Father."

If I had a dollar for every AA member I have heard express a "better idea" for rewriting the Big Book, I would be wealthy. When sensitivity and fairness become more important than the original, accurate, historical record and the truth, we can kiss our vast collective sobriety goodbye.

After twenty years in AA, I have yet to hear a female—either a prospect or proclaimed member—complain about being "wronged" by the basic text of the first third of the AA Big Book. Not one! I have heard numerous female members justly complain about the arrogance and egomania of some male AA members, including myself.

The effectiveness of the AA message is directly dependent on the willingness of the individual to respond to certain spiritual principles. It is a matter of simple individual responsibility!

The writer seems to be practicing selective inclusion and exclusion himself. He includes a sentence from chapter three, paragraph three, that states, "We are convinced to a man that . . . " yet he has excluded the first sentence in that very same paragraph which states, "We alcoholics are men and women who have lost the ability to control our drinking."

While I support any member's right to freedom of expression, I also support any member's right to challenge any material, written or verbal, presented within the framework of the AA Fellowship.

J.S.

Leave the Book Alone
From New York, New York:

WHILE I'M HEARTENED to know that Graham M. is sensitive to the feelings of women and is concerned enough about male-oriented language in our literature to try to change it, I would tell Graham and others to leave the Big Book alone. I'm not a grammarian, but making AA literature gender-neutral or gender-inclusive seems like an unnecessary exercise. Maybe Bill W. didn't consult a lot of women when writing the Big Book because they were still out there getting loaded. When I read AA literature, I feel the spirit of love and fellowship; I don't say to myself, "Gee, that Bill W. was really sexist."

Perhaps a disclaimer at the beginning of the next edition of Alcoholics Anonymous would be nice, but I know that "mankind" means men and women, and would strongly support leaving our basic text as it is.

E.H.

Will It Really Help?
From Flushing, New York:

GRAHAM M.'S ARTICLE reminded me of the times I have attended meetings on the upper east side of Manhattan, where the Third, Seventh, and Eleventh Steps are rewritten and read in a way that makes God sexless (". . . God as we understood God" rather than ". . . God as we understood Him"). While the motive for this revision (to make AA more appealing to women) isn't a bad thing by itself, I get a feeling that I'm not really in an AA meeting when I hear the Steps read that way.

Call me a bleeding deacon if you want, but I find it disconcerting to hear AA literature rewritten to suit the whim of a particular group. Moreover, I can't accept the notion that a gender-free revision of the Big Book, a mostly symbolic act, will really make women feel more at ease in AA. Why not try giving love and service to other alcoholics, regardless of sex?

M.F.

Turning a Blind Eye
From Aptos, California:

I OPENED MY GRAPEVINE tonight thinking about letting my subscription lapse. After a weekend at a women's retreat where we talked about recovery, feminism, and spirituality, I didn't want to wade through the usual pages of "God as we understand Him."

Imagine my surprise and delight when I read Graham M.'s article on the search for more inclusive language. He referred to the gender bias in our beloved—and outdated—text and the blind eye we keep turning to it. Sometimes I feel we leave our brains outside of meetings too often, and base our opinions on fear and habit. Hooray for Graham and those who are willing to rethink our choices, values, and, yes, even our basic text.

It takes courage to see where changes are needed, and courage to keep talking about it. I, for one, plan to keep expressing myself on this and am heartened to hear others feeling the same.

Whether or not Alcoholics Anonymous needs to do a Tenth Step to women for its deep gender bias in its book, I appreciate that at least one member is willing to state it openly. We must do everything we can to make our Fellowship inclusive so female newcomers don't turn away from us because we're too stubborn to see the changes we need to make.

Anonymous

Pertinent at Any Time
From Chicago, Illinois:

WORKS OF LITERATURE, art, and music that survive through time do so not because they adapt to the moment but because they are pertinent at any time. I don't think it's wise to change history to accommodate today's views. As recovering alcoholics, should not our efforts be to change today and thereby change tomorrow's history?

As a gay male, I fully appreciate the limitations of the chapter "To Wives," yet I'd never suggest that it be changed to "To Significant Others" in order to be more relevant to me. It would be nice if the whole world would relate to me, but I feel that such a desire on my part is one reason I landed in AA in the first place.

Sobriety is for those who want it. If I want it badly enough and am willing to go to any length to get it, I will cut through the conventions and get the message.

L.S.

By Men For Men
From Bollene, France:

THREE CHEERS FOR Graham M.! He had the courage to say what this woman alcoholic has felt for a long time: The Big Book was written by men for men.

It isn't just that the language of the text is male-oriented. The entire concept of alcoholism—as presented in the first and subsequent editions—is overwhelmingly masculine. How many alcoholic woman executives identify with "Bill's Story"? What does the Wall Street crash of 1929 mean to a woman stealing six-packs from the supermarket where she works?

Masculine experiences with alcohol dominate chapters one through eleven. The chapter five instructions for taking Step Four—with their emphasis on sexual transgressions—are my particular bête noire. Sexual transgressions? I didn't even think about sex while I was drinking.

In my "Twelve and Twelve" discussion group, I often say that I suggest the Step Four workbook from Al-Anon for women alcoholics to use in taking their Fourth Step. I think it is more realistic for a woman's character defects than the examples given on page 65 of the Big Book.

The men in the group always disagree with me, stating that the Big Book (like the Bible) is for everyone. But the women in the group see my point: The AA program is for everyone but the Big Book speaks mainly to men. Even the text admits this: "With few exceptions, our book thus far has spoken of men" (chapter eight, first paragraph). Chapters eight and nine proceed to set down guidelines for dealing with the alcoholic male and "Dad." The few footnotes regarding women alcoholics and Al-Anon that have been added to the original text simply underscore the attitude that alcoholism is primarily a masculine illness.

Yes, let's do something about the Big Book. Keep the original edition in the archives for historical interest, with its outmoded vocabulary and attitudes of the nineteen-thirties. But please—for today—give us a working text that speaks to all alcoholics.

K.M.

It Works the Way It Is
From Lake Jackson, Texas:

I'M A WOMAN, I've been active in AA for seven years, I have a sponsor, and I sponsor several women. I've never been offended by the focus on men in the Big Book. I've been to meetings all over Texas, in the Midwest, and on the eastern seaboard, and I've never heard a female alcoholic say she had a problem with the language in the Big Book.

Anyone, male or female, can find plenty of ways the Big Book "wrongs" them if they want to, but I truly believe the book was divinely inspired.

R.L.

Chapter 9

❖

IS AA FOR EVERYONE?

Keeping the Doors Open Wide

*E*arly on, it became clear that our growing Fellowship would have to open its doors wider if it was going to offer hope to all alcoholics everywhere. The long form of the Fifth Tradition is simple and to the point: "Our society ought to include all who suffer from alcoholism." The letters in this chapter describe the profound connection we AAs are able to make with one another based solely on our primary purpose—recovery from alcoholism. This connection doesn't overcome or change our individual differences, but it allows us to put them aside so we can help each other.

The Big Book says frankly, "We are people who normally would not mix." It is amazing and wonderful, therefore, that we get along as well as we do—and not only get along, but be of loving service.

❖

Shalom
From Jerusalem, Israel:

THE TWO MOSLEM GENTLEMEN were neatly dressed and very shy; they sat quietly through the entire Friday afternoon meeting of the Jerusalem Shalom AA Group while the rest of us caught up with each other after the trials and celebrations of the Easter/Passover holiday. Our chairman, a young Jew who had come into AA as an alcoholic child, noticed that they hadn't spoken and asked them if they wanted to say anything before the meeting closed.

They did, and despite some difficulty with English, they told their stories. Living far from AA meetings and hesitant to approach the mainly Jewish meetings in Jerusalem, they had gotten sober reading AA books, but now they realized they also needed the fellowship of other alcoholics in order to stay sober. So they gathered their courage and came to ask if they could be part of our meeting.

The response was a heartfelt outpouring of warmth and love, which almost overwhelmed them. We had had Arabic literature waiting for the first people who might need it. A Catholic nurse offered to help set up an Arabic language meeting, and I volunteered to participate since I live on the West Bank. We closed with the Serenity Prayer, which is posted in English, Hebrew, and Arabic in our meeting room, and I stood holding hands with a Moslem on one side and an Orthodox Jew on the other. The Moslems asked for telephone numbers, and nearly everyone in the room gave theirs. When I left, the two men were exchanging numbers with a grizzled Jewish West Bank settler.

I've been reading a lot about AA in North America, where the trend seems to be toward fission: AA for atheists, AA for women, AA for Christians, etc. Here, because we are so few, we move toward fusion. We know we have to hang together in order to remain viable. We have only 400 AA members in all of Israel, two in the Palestine areas, and a couple more in Jordan, both of them Loners. (There must be more drunks in the area—and in fact there are—but with all the division of culture, religion, and ethnicity in our region, reaching out is very limited and difficult.) As a result, we've all needed to learn tolerance and acceptance of one another. We've discovered it can be done and been enriched by the discovery. We've learned that God is indeed operating in Jerusalem meetings and doesn't seem to care much whether we call him God or Allah or HaShem. So why should we? Perhaps this is a lesson that can be used elsewhere, even when the divisions among people are not so great as they are here.

Linda W., October 2000

Kitchen Diplomacy
From Antioch, Illinois:

AS I WAS SITTING at the large group table before my home group began tonight, three young girls walked into the church hall. We had never seen them before and, boy, did they look different. Bless their hearts, they wore sunglasses and had earrings on ears—and noses, tongues, lips. One had a shaved head with a purple mohawk, and another had long pink hair. I have a seventeen-year-old daughter, and even though she doesn't have the dyed hair or earrings, I understood the "statement" these girls were making. People around me were buzzing about how the girls looked.

It turned out to be first the AA meeting for one of the girls, so we got together a First Step meeting for them in the kitchen. There is nothing like talking to newcomers to make me get out of myself. I saw how truly beautiful they looked, and how they listened while the six of us shared our experience, strength, and hope. There were laughter and heads nodding, and when it was their turn to talk, I listened really hard to their stories. One had been ordered by the court because of a citation of driving while intoxicated, and the other two had come because of alcohol and some drug use. We told them about AA's Third Tradition and said that if at this point in their lives they didn't think they needed AA, that was fine—just to not forget about us and come back if their alcohol use progressed. I also told them that alcoholism is the only disease that tells you you're okay while your life is going to hell.

When the meeting ended, we held hands and said the Lord's Prayer. They each got a beginner's kit with our phone numbers and a Big Book. I told the court-ordered girl to start with the stories if the rest seemed too much for her. I learned their names and gave each one a hug.

I saw three young women who were like I used to be—making a statement and trying to survive. I hope they come back. We need them, and I told them that.

Renee F., June 1997

Love and Tolerance
From Missoula, Montana:

THE FIRST PERSON who asked me to sponsor him was a gay man. I had reservations about doing this, since I'm not gay, and I reacted with fear and ignorance. I called my sponsor to get his opinion on the right thing to do. He referred me to Traditions One, Three, Five, and especially Ten. I was reminded that I was to have no opinion on outside issues while acting in my capacity as an AA member.

I continued to work with this man, and thank God I did. I had the privilege of hearing the man's Fifth Step, and thus came to a greater level of understanding. Prior to this occasion, in my own Fifth Step, I'd discovered that I had a resentment against homosexuality. During the course of making my amends, I'd prayed for understanding and to have this resentment removed. But it wasn't until I was able to work with this man that this was accomplished.

Our Big Book states: "Love and tolerance of others is our code." My Higher Power put this person in my life to teach me this wonderful concept and to give me the opportunity to make a living amends.

I've been sober for years and have done Twelfth Step work with a wide variety of people from many backgrounds. I know today that we are all truly perfect children of a loving God, however we choose to define him.

Personal sobriety is an important pursuit in AA, but so is the pursuit of our collective well-being. I'm glad I have a sponsor who gives as much emphasis to the Traditions as to the personal program of recovery.

Justin P., October 2000

One Decent Person
From St. Louis, Missouri:

I'M A SINGLE BLACK MAN, twenty-six years old. I hit bottom in the armed services, where I was sent to in-patient treatment for six weeks. As if it was new to me, I realized that I was a black man! At first I was worried that black people never really get sober. I went to my counselor who was also an AA member. But he had understood my problem before I did.

I'm a big guy—6'2" and 200 pounds—and so was he. When he

saw me in the hall, he'd hug me firmly. I couldn't believe he'd do that. Officers didn't do that; men didn't do that; people of a different race didn't do that. So there I was faced with myself. I said if there is one decent person in the world there may be others. He broke down a wall of isolation that I pray will never return. I am sober four years now.

C.G., December 1991

Loner in the Midst of Us
From Pass Christian, Mississippi:

HERE ON THE GULF COAST of Mississippi, in our very midst, is one who is a "Loner." This is the result not of geography nor of language: She is a Negro. (She also wears an artificial leg, to which she never refers. She never complains or expects special treatment.)

There are at present no integrated groups here. It is not my intent to change local customs, only to ask that AA's warm and loving hand that I have been able to grasp throughout these years be extended to her also, so that she too will come to know the joy of fellowship and know that the road she is traveling is the one of Happy Destiny!

My husband, an engineer, was sent here last year on a temporary assignment. Our recall to California may come at any moment. In view of this it would be unforgivably remiss of me not to make this plea for the Loner in the very midst of us.

M.McD., August 1967

Words to a Loner
From Wellsburg, West Virginia:

I'M WRITING regarding the letter "Loner in the Midst of Us" in the August issue. I wonder how many thinking people have put themselves in that Loner's place. I am a Negro, but I don't think I could have worked the AA program as a Loner, knowing there were many meetings in the area that I couldn't attend. To me, that would have been going from one type of loneliness and frustration to another.

AA to me doesn't mean integration in the sense of bucking the odds to obtain rights that are mine. AA to me means life itself, one day at a time. When I adopt the Serenity Prayer as my guideline, jealousy, hate, resentment, and frustration turn into honesty, purity, unselfishness, and love. I believe that AA and God as I understand him have brought us out of spiritual, mental, and physical decay to become happy and useful people with a purpose: to help the still-suffering alcoholic.

I hope that soon this "Loner" and many others will be tolerated in groups everywhere and—one day at a time—accepted as active members in their groups.

We all know nothing good comes easily.

J.R.N., January 1968

The Right To Be Here
From Riddle, Oregon:

I BELIEVE THAT every AA should say as he enters an AA meeting, "I have a right to be here." Here is the reason for my belief:

Because of some experiences in my early life, I've had for many years the feeling that perhaps I didn't have a right to be here (or there or the other place). Perhaps some might say I had an inferiority complex (which is just about right), but the feeling itself is what I want to talk about, not what its precise name is. Such feelings, I'm told, are to some degree a part of everyone, but in normal people they are so slight as to cause little trouble.

I felt I wanted to have the right to be anywhere, any time, but I also felt I had to make others conscious of my importance as a person before I could gain the desired acceptance. If only I had a little more money, a little better car.

So, after I'd been sober for nearly two years, I got good and drunk one day. It started as I walked by the meeting place, relieved that none of the fellows had seen me, and feeling that a two-bit phony like me had no right to be in an AA meeting.

Then not long ago I sat again in an AA meeting, and for the first time in my life I had the feeling that I really had a right to be somewhere. No, I didn't expect that wonderful feeling to last very long, and it didn't, only a few hours, but I'm willing to wait for it to return, and somehow I believe that through the help of AA and the grace of the greater power, it will.

Bill, April 1955

A Rare Value
From Duluth, Minnesota:

I AM ONE of a handful of openly gay men in the northern area of Minnesota. I have over eighteen years of sobriety, got sober in a major urban area, and have been to AA meetings all over the United States and Canada. I did most of my drinking in one of America's largest gay ghettos. I got sober at a gay AA club. I have also been going to predominantly straight AA meetings since my first week in the Fellowship.

My gay AA group had a lot of discussion about the Third Tradition. Early on, I was told that people had the right to go to any AA meeting they wanted, and what the other attendees at the group felt was their issue, not mine. I don't feel the need to have majority approval of my lifestyle to feel good about myself. When you are a member of a minority, not everyone is going to like you.

Alcoholics Anonymous is probably the only organization in this community that is open to anyone who wishes to attend. Tolerance is a very rare value in our society. AA's policy of tolerance teaches us to deal with our own defects of character and treat other people with respect.

There is a fair degree of prejudice up here. But there is a fair degree of prejudice about a lot of things everywhere. Welcome to the species.

Stephen S., October 2000

Is Our Message for Everyone?
From Lakeland, Florida:

I AM A CHRISTIAN recovering alcoholic. Do I require Christian theology on the podium of my AA meetings in order for me to get sober and stay sober? No, I don't. Do Baptists, Catholics, Republicans, socialists, Democrats, Jews, cops, or robbers require their own particular messages be presented in AA meetings as a stipulation of their recovery from alcoholism? No, they don't.

I find Jesus Christ and the Bible personally meaningful in my life, yet I very seldom mention these things during the meeting because so many people require time and freedom to find their own spiritual path, and because AA's primary purpose constrains me to our major topic. I have learned discretion in matters where there is no complete unity, at least during the meeting. Before and after the meeting I will be as open and daring about my own convictions as I see fit.

When I came into AA, the hand of AA was there for me. That hand was not affiliated with any particular religious denomination, political group, or lifestyle. That hand was simply a recovering alcoholic's hand in mine. Period.

S.A., February 1992

Belonging
From Chicago, Illinois:

IN JANUARY 1985, I'd had enough. I sought out a treatment center in Chicago. During my twenty-eight-day stay, they took me to meetings. I'm of Polish descent and all of my fellow AA attendees were African-American. Afterward, I went to the same meetings that I was introduced to while in treatment, and yes, I was the only nonblack at those meetings.

For my first year in sobriety, these were the meetings I attended. Never once did I receive any more or any less attention than anyone else. I had a mind-boggling situation that I thought was the end of the world, and at times, I thought maybe I didn't belong. When I talked this over with fellow AA members, they suggested I take a personal inventory and try to figure out what was happening to me that had led me to believe I didn't belong. I drew a blank.

Since that first year, I've broadened my horizons. A group of us call Friday night our roaming night because this is when we venture to different meetings in the Chicago and northwest Indiana area. Never once have I been treated as if I didn't belong. And no longer do I think I don't belong.

Fred J., October 2000

Alec
From Edinburgh, Scotland:

A BLIND MAN IS ATTENDING our group here and making good headway, thank God. Alec comes to the meeting with his lovely black Labrador guide dog, Stella (who, incidentally, stands up for the Serenity Prayer).

I wrote to the General Service Office asking for literature in Braille and received a box containing the Braille books—*Alcoholics Anonymous* and *Twelve Steps and Twelve Traditions*—and gave them to Alec. He was quite overwhelmed and could hardly believe it. He couldn't go to bed that night for reading; the excitement was terrific. It was the most marvelous gesture and it has brought immense joy to this man and to all of us here.

Alec lost his sight as a result of war injuries. He says he is very grateful that he was once able to see because he can visualize everything. He says that alcohol was a worse problem than the blindness.

He works as a telephone operator. There is no strain or self-pity in him, and he talks openly about his blindness and tell us what suits him best. What an example of accepting the things we cannot change! His gratitude and enthusiasm are infectious. I took him to a hospital meeting on Sunday where there was another blind chap, sober fourteen days. Alec was thrilled about this contact.

Olive, May 1967

Parallel Paths
From Hamilton, Ontario:

I AM A NORTH AMERICAN NATIVE woman, forty six-years old and sober in AA for three years. I'm grateful to the Creator for allowing me to find AA.

I was raised in a white foster home and always hated my birth mother because of this. When I got sober, I realized that she had died, God rest her soul, as a practicing alcoholic. Because AA taught me forgiveness, I was able to let go of a twenty-year hatred for her.

I am learning more and more about my native culture, and I can see many parallels to AA. AA teaches us to clean house, to become responsible, and to strive to help the still-suffering alcoholic. Native tradition teaches us to know thyself in order to help others, to be responsible, and to help keep the community strong.

God willing, I will continue to learn in AA and continue to learn about my culture. AA has given me back self-respect and dignity. Today I can call myself a lady.

E.O., May 1991

Laughing Again
From Nova Scotia:

I CAN'T SAY I don't see color when I walk into a room. Of course I do. I see brown, yellow, black, and white, and I also see and feel their pain. I was born white because my parents were white, and I was prejudiced because I was raised with prejudice, and I was taught by a wonderful black man how to laugh again.

I was sent directly from detox to the twenty-eight-day program available in our city's mental hospital, and I was a very angry woman.

I had no idea I'd stored up so much anger and resentment in my system. The residents were each given duties on the floor, and mine was the kitchen.

I had yet to learn about gratitude (I could have had the job of cleaning the toilets). It seemed to me that each and every one of these alcoholics were out to get me, and were dirtying as many cups as they could find. As soon as I washed them up, they walked by and took another clean one. Finally I exploded, and yelled that I had better things to do than clean their coffee cups, and if they dirtied any more than their original morning cup, they could damn well wash it themselves.

I didn't realize it then, but those people were hurting and were just as full of anger and resentment as I was, and when I exploded at them, I gave them a target to direct their anger at. So hell was born in the recovery kitchen. I was deluged with dirty coffee cups. One day a black hand reached for a cup on the drain board, and in tears, I slapped it. What I didn't see was the towel he held under the stump of his other arm and the smile on his face.

His name was Billy, and for the first time in a long time there was laughter back in my life. He could have been a stand-up comedian. I don't think Billy knew he was hilarious. He just was.

Mornings we had to show up for yoga, and Billy would come out of his room, hair not combed, shirt buttoned wrong, and it was obvious he had just rolled out of bed at the last minute. We had to do some deep breathing while lying on mats on the floor. Billy would go back to sleep immediately and snore. My mat was usually next to his, and I would burst out laughing. It felt so good to laugh again. He gave me back my sense of humor, and a lot of my anger disappeared.

Billy couldn't read or write, and every night he would help me with the dishes, then drag a small sofa into a quiet corner, and I would help him with his assignments for that night. My mind was still foggy from alcohol, so by reading out loud to Billy, I also learned. I would never have absorbed what I needed to if I didn't have to answer his questions, and I no doubt would have nodded off if I had been reading to myself. I might never have made it into AA if it hadn't been for Billy's helping hand.

When you practice prejudice, you lose so much. The journey we're all on wasn't designed by Bill W. and Dr. Bob for one race only.

It was designed for alcoholics who are willing to go to any lengths to become what our Higher Power has planned for us.

Joan M., October 2000

May I Never Repeat Those Words
From Reno, Nevada:

I FIRST WALKED INTO an AA meeting when I was twenty-one years old. The members were all middle-aged and had been good, hard drinkers. They told me I wasn't old enough to be an alcoholic. So I continued on my merry drinking ways.

About five or six years later, I was tired of my drinking and wanted to quit, so I went back to AA. This time there were more members and younger ones, so I was able to get sober and stay that way for about seven years; but for the last five of those seven I didn't go to meetings, because there was discord along with the usual remarks from the older ones: "We don't think you are an alcoholic."

I kept in touch with some of the members, but I started drinking again. For four years, I made life hell for my family and almost lost them. I'm surprised that they stayed around. We moved three or four times, and last year I contacted AA again; I went to one meeting, and my contact said he would pick me up for the next meeting, as I had no way to get there. I never saw him again. So I continued drinking.

This week I went to the meeting on my own. I was told that they didn't think I was an alcoholic last year and they still thought that way. I would like to get sober and stay sober. I know I can't do it on my own; this is why AA has always called me back. I have a drinking problem, and I think I'm an alcoholic!

Groups wonder why some members don't stay sober very long. How can they when they hear: "We don't think you are an alcoholic?" If I ever get sober, may I never repeat those words to someone who is looking for help.

L.D.S., September 1969

God As We Understand Him
From Colombo, Ceylon:

THE PREDOMINANT RELIGION here is Buddhism. I am proud to say, as a recovered Buddhist alcoholic, that Bill and Bob deserve praise and honor for having so thoughtfully laid down the Twelve Steps of the Alcoholics Anonymous program. In fact, these Steps embody the very principles upon which the Buddhist philosophy is also built, though of course worded differently. Unless we discipline ourselves, we never can become victorious.

Anonymous, February 1968

Unconditional Love

From North Charleston, South Carolina:

I'VE HEARD PEOPLE in AA rooms share that the moment they walked into their first meeting they knew they belonged. But that's not how it was for me. I'm thirty-eight years old and a black woman alcoholic. I went to my first AA meeting alone after coming out of a thirty-day treatment center. I walked in, got a cup of coffee, and found a seat. There were three or four men (white) standing around talking. None of them acknowledged my presence. Another man entered and started telling them about his day's work. I don't think he noticed me sitting there and he started talking about some guy he worked with and referred to the man as a "nigger." It is not necessary to say how I felt. I hung on to my seat. I read Tradition Three on the wall which says "the only requirement for AA membership is a desire to stop drinking." I know more than anything else I had a desire not to drink.

All sorts of crazy ideas went through my mind. I'm from New York City and I'd heard all kinds of horror stories about the South while I was growing up. I didn't know if I'd be taken out to be hung from a tree or what. But I did know I was willing to go to any lengths to stay sober. So I sat through that meeting, terrified. At the end of the meeting, everyone held hands, said the Lord's Prayer, and chanted "Keep coming back." So I did.

Some time later, one of those men from the first meeting introduced me to service work and I have come to love all of them, even the one who made the racial remark. Today I feel that I belong. I have made this group my home group. Everyone shows me unconditional love and no one notices what color I am. I sponsor several women (white), and I am the secretary of the group.

I learned a couple of lessons that first day: First, some of us are sicker than others but we are all children of God, and we have the right to be right and the right to be wrong. Second, I'll always greet a newcomer with love and understanding, because I know how it feels to come to the last house on the block and not be welcomed.

K.J., September 1991

Plea for the Handicapped
From Rockledge, Florida:

I JOINED AA one year ago, after miserable years of depending on booze. I thoroughly enjoy going to meetings—the wonderful fellowship and quality sobriety. When visiting other cities, I enjoy meetings there.

One thing disturbs me, however: Many meeting places are not accessible to the handicapped. I recently visited another state, where I had to climb three flights of stairs to get to a meeting. Even though I'm not disabled, I have worked for years with the handicapped and am aware that there are many problem drinkers among them.

Those in wheelchairs, with heart or lung trouble, and many senior citizens need easy access to meetings and AA central offices. This may require choosing ground-level locations, or buildings with ramps, elevators, and rest rooms equipped for those in wheelchairs. This consideration should also be kept in mind when choosing locations for AA conferences, conventions, and assemblies, to help disabled people wanting to attend.

I'd also like to recommend that when meeting books are made up, meeting locations that offer accessibility to the handicapped should be pointed out in some way. And at a recent meeting, it was suggested that group Twelfth Step lists should note members who have special talents or expertise in dealing with handicapped persons, such as the deaf.

AA is a great life for me, and I don't want anyone who needs it and wants it to be left out.

B.C., April 1982

Strength In Diversity
From Pittsburg, Texas:

I'M A BLACK MALE, age fifty-four. I used and abused alcohol from my teenage years until a year ago. My past is littered with the debris of broken dreams, ruined plans, broken marriages, prisons, jails, car wrecks, and mental hospitals. For years I foundered in a living hell of despair and depression, confusion and remorse, erratic behavior and shame. Nameless anxiety was my constant companion, and I lost my ability to laugh fully and freely.

My last drunk was a horror to end all horrors. My personality split—one part urged me to end it all, and another urged me to hold on.

While in this state I was able to reach an older black man, a friend who had introduced me to AA back in 1978. He understood my condition and kept me with him until my wife's minister carried me to an area treatment center. In treatment, I received intensive therapy, education about this disease of alcoholism, and was reintroduced to AA.

Since my discharge from treatment, I have attended meetings regularly, formed a close relationship with my sponsor, worked on the Steps, and been consistent in prayer and meditation.

I now have a year of sobriety in AA. My life has taken a 180-degree turn. I can see and feel the richness and beauty of my life. I take the time to savor the day-by-day blessings that come into my life. I can accept with some degree of humility the pain, grief, and disappointments that come to me as a part of the human condition. I believe that life is good, and to be happy and to laugh are not cardinal sins. My alcoholism, once a curse, has become a blessing.

I cherish the support of my Higher Power, treasure the support of a good wife who is a devoted Al-Anon, and am amazed that I have two beautiful children and quite a few friends, white, black, and Hispanic. A measure of gratitude lives with me daily. I sometimes think that I could be on an early sobriety high, but even if I am, I intend to keep carrying the AA message.

L.T., April 1991

The Gift of Equality
From Morristown, New Jersey:

I WAS RECENTLY ASKED to speak at an AA special interest group, a gay AA meeting to be exact. Special interest groups, as AA history tells us, were supported by Bill W. early on, specifically to meet the needs of the women coming into AA. I was thrilled to be able to meet this commitment but was disappointed when I couldn't get anyone to go with me because they didn't want to go to that particular meeting. I didn't have to be gay to attend that meeting, all I needed was the desire to stop drinking, and I have that every day.

I left that meeting feeling like I had met new friends. I have since been back because that meeting offers me unity, service, and fellowship. I've met a group of people who have what I want, and I'm willing to go to any lengths to get it. Our trips to the diner are hilarious and fun-filled. I have never felt so good in all of my life.

I used to live a life of ridicule and judgment against any and all beings, but AA has taught me to ask, Who am I to judge? I sat on too many barstools feeling less than other people; I don't need to come into AA and start feeling superior. I treasure the gift of equality that AA has given me.

M.B., May 1991

Repaying the Generosity
Via E-mail:

I'M A TWENTY-SEVEN-YEAR-OLD, white, Irish, Catholic Vermonter, who is studying law in Boston. Because of Tradition Ten ("Alcoholics Anonymous has no opinion on outside issues; hence the AA name ought never be drawn into public controversy") none of this excludes me from membership in Alcoholics Anonymous.

I finally admitted that I was powerless over alcohol and that my life was unmanageable when I was living in Senegal, West Africa, for two years. During my first year of sobriety, I kept sober through correspondence with other alcoholics in Europe, South America, the South Pacific, and the United States. Thus I do not have a conventional American-culture view of Alcoholics Anonymous. But I am still allowed to remain a member of Alcoholics Anonymous because of the Twelve Traditions.

During a meeting of Alcoholics Anonymous, I don't identify my ethnic heritage nor my religion. I save that sort of information for my sponsor. A sponsor is the person I go to for personal work on my spiritual condition. Meetings are for fellowship. The "Twelve and Twelve" states: ". . . one old-timer recently declared, 'Practically never have I heard a heated religious, political, or reform argument among AA members. So long as we don't argue these matters privately, it's a cinch we never shall publicly.'"

I don't want to talk about religion at a meeting of Alcoholics Anonymous. I don't speak of those without religious affiliations as "heathens"; in mutual respect, I hope that others will not refer to my religion as though it were a disease that one needs to recover from. Each time I hear "I'm a recovering Catholic" at an AA meeting, I question whether or not I'm really welcome. I usually pray for the person. I always feel uncomfortable.

On page 87 of *Alcoholics Anonymous*, we are given some guidance concerning this issue of spirituality and religion. This seems like a good place to keep the discussion: "If we belong to a religious denomination which requires a definite morning devotion, we attend to that also. If not members of religious bodies, we sometimes select and memorize a few set prayers which emphasize the principles we have been discussing. There are many helpful books also. Suggestions about these may be obtained from one's priest, minister, or rabbi. Be quick to see where religious people are right. Make use of what they offer."

Alcoholics Anonymous owes a lot to religious people. Father Edward Dowling, Reverend Sam Shoemaker of the Oxford Group, and Sister Ignatia all played important parts in the formation of AA and in the lives of our two principal founders. We might not exist were it not for the charity of these and others. The best way we can repay their generosity is to extend that same generosity to others. Let us hope, pray, and take action to ensure that AA remains a haven for all alcoholics, whether affiliated with religious groups or not.

Jim, May 2000

At Home in AA
From San Francisco, California:

WHEN I GOT SOBER, I wondered whether I could fit into AA. As a gay man, I brought with me many self-centered fears about what others would think "if they only knew." Overall, however, my experiences have been positive, and now I feel more comfortable being open and honest about myself in AA than in the "outside world."

One particular event helped me. I traveled to Fresno, California, for some service work. Some people there knew I was gay, while others did not. I asked for a local meeting schedule — I wanted a gay meeting but was afraid to be honest about it. When one of the men in the group gave me the schedule, he said, "Someone told me you were gay, so I underlined some gay meetings for you. A couple of guys from my home group told me these are good meetings." I was touched by this gesture. It helped me to understand that I can share in the experience of seeing a fellowship grow up around me in AA, whether I am gay or straight.

B.C., November 1992

Blacks in AA
From Geneva, New York:

I'VE BEEN CONCERNED about our black members who are so often just passing through. The idea that we are unique or different is a rationalization for many dropouts. I was different also, but stayed around long enough to find out that AA could work for me. Now, being different is part of the fabric that keeps AA vital and me growing. And I'm not so different after all.

I want you to know what perhaps you haven't seen. Early in my sobriety, I heard a staunch AA member make a racial comment (not a slur, just an awkward and unnecessary addition) in the presence of a new black member. I was livid! No one seemed upset but me.

I wound up doing some fast sorting through of my thoughts. My decision was not to further embarrass our new member by confronting the issue there. But—and it's a big but—I made a commitment then which I have to the best of my ability carried through for over six years: I make a point immediately, whenever there is an unfamiliar black face, to introduce myself and welcome the individual. And if I hear any comment that I consider racially sensitive, I will talk privately with the member who makes it.

The staunch member of long ago, when I confronted him after the meeting, didn't agree with my point. But I had the satisfaction of knowing that I had not remained guilty, where silence means compliance.

Someday AA will be as representative as the non-discriminating disease itself is—look at the history of women's participation in AA over fifty years.

But for now, keep coming back and welcome home.

R.H., January 1986

Welcome
From Antwerp, Belgium:

MANY YEARS AGO, one of our Jewish members, whom we'll call Mark, became friends with an AA member who had immigrated from Germany and ran a garage specializing in Volkswagens. The Jewish member, new to the program, attended an AA lunch group and said to his German friend, whom we'll call Hans: "You know, I'm Jewish."

"Is that so?" said Hans, busily eating away in the European two-handed way.

"Yes," said Sid, "and Jews are almost never alcoholics."

"Oh?" said Hans, chewing away. "That's interesting."

"So," said Sid, "maybe I'm not alcoholic."

Hans looked up briefly and said, "*Ja*, and maybe you're not Jewish!" Over the years, this became one of Sid's favorite stories.

Our small group is English-speaking, started by Belgians in English for English speakers. Sometimes in the early days, the only one present was our secretary, a Belgian, who kept the meeting alive just in case a traveling Brit or Yank dropped by. Today we have two new members: One is Jewish, a slim young female veteran of the Israeli army; the other is a pleasant young man named Ali. Other nationalities represented around the table last week included the United Kingdom, the United States, Germany, and Belgium.

Not too long ago, our meeting became nonsmoking with a smoke break at the break. This was in recognition of health conditions within the group that have kept some members away. Because this is the only group we English speakers have here, because we need AA to get and stay sober, everyone, indeed, is most truly welcome. And each new member has that much more assurance that our little gang will still be meeting here next Tuesday.

Taylor C., October 2000

AA's Universal Language
From Santa Cruz, California:

OUR GROUP HAS gratefully received three AA pamphlets in Chinese from the General Service Office for my pigeon Charlie Y., the only Chinese AA member in Northern California.

We love him so in our Downtown Group here in Santa Cruz. Charlie participates in every group function. He is not only an ex-pilot of the Flying Tigers but a gourmet cook and has cooked the most delightful dishes from his native China for our potluck dinners on the third Saturday each month.

He is truly an AA miracle. Three months ago, you wouldn't have given him any chance of making this program. With the help of Buddha and his fellow AA members, he stuck with us, and now he's the most popular fellow in the group, which numbers over seventy members.

Without my AA membership, I would never have had the friendship and inspiration of Charlie Y.

Alice H., February 1974

Expensive Unhappiness
From Kansas City, Missouri:

I'M TWENTY YEARS OLD. Looking back, I see that I was an alcoholic at fifteen, when I took my first drink. The boys I ran around with drank for the fun of it and to be smart—but always stopped before they had too much. I drank because I liked the effects of alcohol, and I never knew when to quit. I always wound up drunk. At fifteen, I spent my first night in jail for being drunk.

When I was seventeen, I heard of AA but did nothing about it. When I was nineteen, I finally came into AA, and only through the Fellowship have I been able to gain self-respect, happiness, and a confidence in the future.

There are many young people—younger than myself—who need AA. If they will give it a chance to work for them, they will save themselves many years of sickness, despair, and expensive unhappiness.

Every day I ask God to help me overcome my impetuousness and devil-may-care attitude and imbue in me a sense of gratitude for the wonderful blessing of sobriety I have received.

P.S., October 1948

Genuine Healing
From Wilson, North Carolina:

I'M A WHITE MALE with nearly sixteen years of sobriety and active involvement in AA. I came to AA in 1975 after having spent two years as a homeless, angry, fear-ridden, defeated man.

Great things have happened to me since the day I came to AA. I was married on my second AA birthday to a woman I met in AA. The judge who married us was also an AA member. We have two beautiful, healthy, lively daughters who have never seen their parents drunk. The AA program, when practiced as a way of life, is more powerful than the disease of alcoholism.

When drinking, however, I was involved in some serious hatred regarding the black race. As my alcoholism progressed, so did the hatred. As a result of my alcoholism and this hatred, I was responsible for the death of a human being. Not an easy thing to live with when sober.

However, God's grace through the power of AA is always equal to whatever the problem or defect might be. Some years ago, because of AA, I was thrown into close interaction with a black man who had spent many years in prison and had a lifetime of alcoholism and hating white folks. As we became better acquainted, it was easy to see that our individual experiences involving alcoholism, hatred, and fear were nearly identical.

We became increasingly good friends over the years, sharing much Fifth-Step type material. Today Jimmy is one of the closest friends I have, and I believe I am equally close to his heart.

Because of the power of the principles of AA, we have transcended the defects of racism and hatred. Genuine healing has in fact taken place for both of us.

Powerful business, this AA program.

S.M., April 1991

Another Minority Group
From Winter Park, Florida:

I USED TO THINK, a few years ago, that I would like to be a member of a minority group. It seemed that, though they suffered discrimination and prejudice, they had purpose, and each member always had someone on his side—his fellows.

Then I did become a member of a minority group: I became a practicing alcoholic. As a member of this group, I knew discrimination and prejudice; I was socially unacceptable; my physical presence caused discomfort in those around me.

There was no single cataclysmic event that drove me to seek help—just a soul-sickness so desperate there was no longer any living with it. A few attempts to end it all resulted in humiliating frustration and costly hospital stays. I'd exhausted the patience of family and friends. I'd consulted with doctors and lied about my condition and habits. I'd slammed every door that was open to me. Except one.

So I became a member of another minority group. I joined the Fellowship of Alcoholics Anonymous, where the members have a purpose, where they are united to conquer a common foe and make a better world.

E.G., October 1971

Chapter 10

❖

YOUR MOVE: SEPTEMBER 2002

Should We Go Easy on the God Stuff?

*S*hould we go easy on the God stuff?" That was the
question one writer asked in an article published in the April
2002 issue. He examined the assumption that we should
never "soft-peddle AA's core principle"—a belief in God or
a Higher Power. He wrote that in the area where he lived
"the people in meetings most interested in talking about their
God . . . fervently believe they possess the exclusive ticket to
salvation, and that you are doomed unless you share their
beliefs. . . . Their parochial presentation of God lacks the
ecumenical view outlined by Bill W. that is the foundation of
Alcoholics Anonymous." He went on to quote chapter four
of the Big Book, "We Agnostics": "When, therefore, we speak
to you of God, we mean your own conception
of God. This applies, too, to other spiritual
expressions which you find in this book."
Grapevine readers were willing
and eager to answer the question
that he posed.

❖

Which God? Which?

From Virginia Beach, Virginia:

SOMETIME DURING THE WINTER of 1995, I was attending a three-speaker AA meeting at one of the old clubhouses in Brooklyn. That night, the first speaker started out by saying how praying to God had helped him get sober. He had barely begun his story when a young man sitting up front interrupted and asked, "Which God?" At first, the speaker ignored him, but no sooner did he try to continue than the man interrupted again. "Which God?" he demanded. Taken aback, the speaker asked, "What do you mean, 'Which God?' God is God." The young man became increasingly agitated, repeatedly asking, "Which God? Which God?"

At this point, the speaker became visibly angry, thinking the guy was some kind of troublemaker. I was starting to think the same. When the speaker asked him to please stop interrupting, the young man became frantic, desperately asking, "Which God? Which God do I pray to?"

Then we began to realize that, judging by his accent and attire, the young man had probably recently come from the Indian subcontinent. Apparently at his first AA meeting, he just didn't know the usual meeting "etiquette." Perhaps he even thought he was attending an alcoholism class and assumed it was acceptable to interrupt the speaker, who, after all, was sitting up front at a desk.

Whatever the case may have been, we obviously weren't going to be able to continue until we dealt with his question, so the group started trying to help him. "Do you believe in God?" someone asked. "Which God? Which God?" he answered.

Finally someone else asked, "Do you have more than one God?"

"Yes!" the man replied. "Which one do I have to pray to, to get sober?"

Aha! He was a polytheist. Not knowing what his choices were, we kicked the problem around for a minute until someone asked, "Do you have a God to pray to when you are ill, a God who helps you get well?"

"Yes," he replied, nodding vigorously. He even told us the name of the God, although I couldn't make it out.

"Well, pray to that God," someone suggested.

Suddenly, a big smile broke across his face. "Okay. I will pray to __." (Once again, I couldn't make out the name.) "Thank you, thank you!" he exclaimed, and the meeting proceeded.

That young man seemed very anxious to do whatever it took to get sober. He just needed to understand the instructions in a way that made sense to him.

Larry M.

What Works for Me
From Denton, Texas:

IN RESPONSE TO "Should We Go Easy on the God Stuff?": I was not surprised but amused. The author quotes the passage from the Big Book that tells us to "stress the spiritual feature" and then complains because someone is not doing it the way he feels it should be done.

I thought a meeting was a place to share our experience, strength, and hope. If my experience is with a God whom I call Jesus, then why shouldn't I share that? It doesn't force the word *Jesus* on anyone; it just allows others to know what has worked for me. I don't flash the name to beat others over the head; rather, I rely on my relationship with my Higher Power to lead and direct what I am saying, which includes using his name on occasion.

The main purpose of the Big Book is to enable us to find a power greater than ourselves. Step Eleven is there so that our God continues to grow and our principles grow into a working relationship with the God of our understanding.

Others can present their experiences without it seeming as if we're in a competition. One hopes that this adds to the different perspectives brought into meetings and allows others to identify and chose from those who have what they want. Most of us sense that real tolerance of others' shortcomings and viewpoints and respect for their opinions are attitudes which make us more useful to others.

May we all seek to understand rather than to be understood.

Christy S.

The Practice of Prayer
From St. Louis, Missouri:

AA IS NOT a religious organization, but occasionally I observe many in our Fellowship doing things that, at the very least, confuse the newcomer or perpetuate the general public's misconceptions of us. At our state AA convention last year, I saw a small group of AA members on their knees, reciting the Third Step prayer in a hotel hallway. They were in full view of another organization using the same hotel. The same religious practice can be seen at many regular AA meetings, both closed and open to the public.

The Board of Probation and Parole in my state has kept our message of recovery from being heard by issuing more than one judgment based upon the possible negative consequences of "mixing church and state." This is an unfortunate situation that has been aggravated by those of us who insist on publicly mixing our brand of Christianity with Alcoholics Anonymous.

As a recovering agnostic, I believe that God, if he exists, must be the highest power there is. However, AA simply suggests that I recognize there is a power greater than I am. For me, any AA group is a power greater than I am, and as a responsible member, I should abide by the group conscience and not try to change our Fellowship into a religious organization.

Glenn P.

The God Thing
From Atlanta, Georgia:

NEAR THE END of my very first AA meeting fourteen years ago, I was invited to share. I'd liked much of what I'd heard and said so. Then I pointed to the Steps and said, "But I'm going to have trouble with the God thing." That offended a young man who'd apparently found religion in AA. He verbally abused me for ten minutes.

The discussion leader apologized and urged me to return. I did the next day and remained quiet for the entire hour. The young man launched another tirade in my direction, saying something akin to, "You'd better find God or you won't even come close to sobriety." I stayed away from AA for nine years and came close to dying during that time. Fortunately, I did come back, and the Fellowship—which has served as my higher power most of the time—saved my life.

Stephen B.

Go Easy? Not Me
From Manchester, New Hampshire:

I THOUGHT I would answer the rhetorical question on the cover of the April issue, "Should We Go Easy on the God Stuff?" My vote is no.

The Big Book talks about my problem by saying, "If, when you honestly want to, you find you cannot quit entirely, or if when drinking, you have little control over the amount you take, you are probably alcoholic. If that be the case, you may be suffering from an illness which only a spiritual experience will conquer."

After years of doing it my way, baffling my doctors, and finally finding a solution, I need no more convincing. And now, after having had a spiritual awakening as the result of the Steps, I try to carry this message to other alcoholics and to practice these principles in all my affairs.

Let the rehabs go easy on the God stuff. I have too much to lose.

Dave R.

The *Neti, Neti*
From Billings, Montana:

WHEN I ENTERED treatment, the last thing I wanted was for anybody to push anything at me that looked remotely like religion. The use of the word "God" in the Twelve Steps was disheartening enough. Now, after six years of sobriety, I've begun to discern the subtle differences between religion and personal spirituality. As I once heard someone say, "I'm comfortable with using the word *God* now that I have absolutely no idea what it is I'm talking about." My conception of my Higher Power is a lot like the *neti, neti* ("not this, not this") of Vedanta.

I was lucky enough to find a home group that was understanding and supportive of my struggles with faith and God and always open to spiritual insight, regardless of the source. Like the author of "Should We Go Easy on the God Stuff?," I don't think I would have stuck around if not for the patience and tolerance of my fellows in AA who have let me search out my own path.

Dave W.

More, Not Less
From Midvale, Utah:

MORE OF GOD is not something to fear. It is, on the contrary, something that suggests more splendor, more beauty, more wonder, more mystery, more adventure, more investigation, more questioning, more wisdom, more peace, more love, more grace, more joy, more commitment, more faith, more hope, and more courage. There is no end to more of God.

Is AA God's instrument of grace or is God AA's instrument? Our Second Tradition says God is the ultimate authority. Another word for "ultimate" is absolute. God either is or he isn't. The collective conscience of our founders seems to say that he is. So let's not dilute his name or deny his presence by suggesting he is a lightbulb or doorknob or something less than he is, or, because of our success, think we need him less today than yesterday.

We are sixty-seven years sober [in 2002] as a Fellowship. It's time to open our ears to Bill W.'s greatest fear—AA's success. As we continue to grow and prosper, let's not get so absorbed in our accomplishments that we forget our humble beginnings. The birth of AA is proof that when we are dissatisfied, when we are weak, when we are failures in ourselves—then God can come in. My prayer for AA and what I believe to be our common welfare is for more of God and less of Alcoholics Anonymous, that our very program would become more anonymous.

T. S.

A Zone of One's Own
From Fort Lauderdale, Florida:

I TOOK A FEW MOMENTS to take a rough count: The word *God* appears fifty-nine times in the March Grapevine. It appears sixty-nine times in the April Grapevine. So, to answer the question put forth in the April issue, I am definitely inclined to say, "Yes, we should go easy on the God stuff."

I am concerned at the intrusion of religion into the framework of AA meetings—for example, the Lord's Prayer recitation. I, therefore, try to avoid meetings where this recitation is used. I think that if our members have a religion they believe is enhancing their quality of life, I'm all for it. But please do not inject your religion into my AA.

Fortunately, here in south Florida we have AA meetings that are free-thinker meetings, and for the most part, "God-free zones." I like that.

Richard H.

The Real Deal
From Baton Rouge, Louisiana:

THE "GOD STUFF" is difficult for some of us. The Big Book refers to this and also tells us not to shy away from it. So we talk about it. But how? For me, it's at best a little awkward and at worst very difficult to discuss spirituality in completely generic terms.

I'm a devout, lifelong Catholic. That is an integral part of my experience, strength, and hope. I call my Higher Power "God" and do not feel I should have to qualify that every time I speak at a meeting with "whom I choose to call God" or anything else. I'm perfectly okay with others referring to Buddha, Mohammed, Yahweh, or whatever name they call their Higher Power. I'm uncomfortable with anyone citing the Bible, the Koran, the Talmud, or any non-AA literature as the truth in an AA meeting. But I certainly give them the right to refer to or even quote (briefly) from any of these if it's part of their sober experience. I downright dislike anyone saying theirs is the only way, as much as I dislike anyone saying in an AA meeting that they are a "recovering Catholic" or "recovering Baptist."

In my eighteen years of recovery, I have heard all this and more —way more!—and I probably will again. My dealing with it has taken many shapes. Sometimes, it's "love and tolerance of others"; sometimes, it's working through a resentment; sometimes it's a group conscience thing.

So far I haven't found it necessary to take a drink over any of it, and more than once, it has caused me to experience spiritual growth. And that's the deal, isn't it?

Colleen F.

Chapter 11

❖

RITUAL AT MEETINGS

Exploring What Works

$\mathcal{V}$ery few references to meetings appear in the first 164 pages of the Big Book, probably because AA was only three years old when the book was written, and meetings—small groups of people gathering in someone's home—were just beginning to form, primarily in Ohio and New York. So there's not much guidance we can get from our primary text on the format of meetings. And, of course, AA doesn't lay down rules for such things: The Fourth Tradition says, "Each group should be autonomous except in matters affecting other groups or AA as a whole." However, this is an important matter, since meetings are an integral part of many AA members' program of recovery. The letters that follow express some of the viewpoints on how a meeting should best be conducted to support our primary purpose and our spiritual way of life.

❖

Distractions
From Vancouver, British Columbia:

THERE'S A TREND in AA meetings around this city that has left me feeling vaguely uncomfortable. This is the notion of "reward" through the giving of chips.

A friend was telling me about an experience he had at a meeting that gives out these bits of plastic or metal. He said a new woman wasn't feeling strong enough to go up to the secretary to collect her newcomer chip and so refused it. After the meeting, a few people tried to coerce her into taking this chip, but no one spent the time explaining to her the idea behind it (if there is one). My friend then asked the newcomer if she had a directory of meetings, to which she said no. When he tried to find one for her, he discovered with dismay there wasn't a meeting book in the whole place.

It occurs to me we may have forgotten that sobriety—freedom from alcohol—is the sole purpose of an AA group. We are not in the business of "rewarding" drunks for coming to AA. The idea behind the chip system, or birthday celebration, was to remind us to humbly remember where we came from and that we are sober today through the grace of God and the Twelve Steps. It was never intended to replace the teaching of the Twelve Steps, but it appears that's what is happening. We're so busy falling over the new person to give him or her some sort of token that we forget to give the only thing we really have: our sobriety. Can we please get back to the basics of informing new people that they have been given a way to stay sober, through the practice of the Twelve Steps?

When I got to my first meeting, I was given several AA pamphlets and a meeting directory with the phone numbers of group members in it. I went home to study this thing called Alcoholics Anonymous, and thus began my journey fifteen-plus years ago. I'm not saying that this is the only way to be introduced to this Fellowship, but I'm concerned that we are becoming distracted from our primary purpose.

V.E., January 1992

Greasing the Path
From Lincoln, Nebraska:

HAVING VISITED MANY of our local meetings, I found that there is no set pattern to any of them. I did notice, however, that those meetings that had very little ritual generally tended to stray away from the subject of alcoholism and recovery, if they approached it at all.

The more stable meetings, in my opinion, usually opened with a moment of silence, then a reading from the Big Book and sometimes a Tradition. This seems to get our thinking on the track of why we're at the meeting.

Generally speaking, I don't think there is too much ritual in our meetings. I would say we should continue to study our literature and use a little common sense. If I were truly concerned, I could bring it up at my meeting, always keeping in mind that each group can run its meetings however it wants to, as long as it doesn't affect another meeting or AA as a whole.

David S., February 1991

Ritual in AA
From Islip Terrace, New York:

WHEN I CAME TO AA twenty-three years ago at the age of twenty-three, I stayed because the old-timers stressed that I didn't have to believe in anything and I didn't have to conform to anyone or anything. This I could buy.

I remember an old-timer who looked like W.C. Fields saying to me, "Kid, this program works if you let it—but remember, to thine own self be true. You are responsible for you."

As time went on and people came out of rehab programs and as some people rejoined their religion, a slow pattern of holding hands, hugging, and a sort of have-to prayer pattern developed.

I've seen many young people in AA, and while I think that hand-holding and hugging is good in one way, I also think it detracts from what I was taught.

Today I get the impression there's a notion that if I just go to a meeting, "share" what's on my mind or how I'm feeling, and then leave, I'm cured for the day. This is a fallacy.

M.O., July 1991

Playing Tag
From New York, New York:

REGARDING AN INCREASED tendency toward ritual in AA, I am concerned about the tags that have been added to the Serenity Prayer at meeting's end. At first it was "Keep coming back." Not that this isn't a loving (though somewhat impersonal) bit of encouragement, but it began a can-you-top-this routine which next had people shouting "It works!" True enough. But once there were no objections to this tagline, the rote quickly expanded to "It works if you work it"—with one or two unabashed exhibitionists yelling their own "So work it!"

Which is just the point where I want to leave the meeting, because it strikes me that this jingoism departs from the principles of AA. As I understand it, AA works if I let it—not if I work it. I need a daily reminder that my working anything never worked. Now, I admit I'm powerless. Now, I surrender. Now, as Step Seven suggests, I ask God to do the "work."

When I first came to the rooms of AA, my mind was so muddled I could barely learn the correct order of those gentle words in the Serenity Prayer that ask for God's grace. It seems reasonable that we avoid making it longer to memorize, and that we're careful not to add directives having the faint odor of rules and regulations. We're beginning to sound like a revival meeting.

Anonymous, February 1991

The Content Not the Container
From Moore, Oklahoma:

I'VE BEEN IN A LOT of meetings and the ritual in each has its own unique style based on its group history. I've been in meetings where the blue card regarding singleness of purpose was always read and in those where it was not. In meetings where we did or did not say the Lord's Prayer (with and without hand-holding). Where the Responsibility Declaration was read. Where, in order to speak, you had to give your sobriety date (and if you had changed that date, you had to explain what happened). Where a variety of passages from the Big Book were read before and after the meeting. Where everyone sat in a circle, or in rows, or around tables, where the person to speak had to stand, had to wait to be called on, or was called on by rotation, *etcetera*.

All of these have kept me sober. I never complained about getting my booze in a dirty glass and was happy with any of the drinking rituals that got me into the space between mellow and comatose. I don't see the ritual or its lack as anything other than a way to open and close a meeting. The content is more important than the container or the ritual. I'm willing to go to any lengths today to get sober so I'll suit up and show up at any meeting I can find with or without ritual. As Tradition Four says, each group is autonomous to do its thing. My thing is to show up.

Donald A., February 1991

What Happened to Simplicity?
From Maui, Hawaii:

I USED TO ENJOY meetings that started with a moment's silence and reading of the Preamble, followed by the discussion. Now, I find myself at meetings that start with a moment's silence, the Serenity Prayer, "How It Works," the Preamble, and the introduction of new-comers and visitors. During the meeting, people are obliged to intro-duce themselves by name every time they say something, followed by the obligatory "Hi, Joe!" The meetings end with the reading of the Traditions, announcements, passing the basket, and the Lord's Prayer, in a circle, with hands held. Whatever happened to keeping it simple?

Tradition Three states: "The only requirement for AA member-ship is a desire to stop drinking." Refuse to say the Lord's Prayer or "How It Works" and see if this is true.

I have ten years of sobriety and am fully aware of increased ritu-alization. Where does it all end? Where it will end for many of us is where it has ended for many others who have freed themselves from the confines of strict, cult-type involvements: in the true freedom of sober, sane, fulfilled productive individuals, who have walked out, not dropped out.

M.S., February 1991

Too Much Ritual
From Greenwich, Connecticut:

INFORMALITY HAS BEEN the key element of welcome at AA meeting ever since Bill W. and his fellow drunks went on their own. They rec-ognized that love and acceptance best streaked through meetings bereft of precious religiosities, awesome intonements, and readings from hallowed books. Absence of form has played a large part in convincing newcomers of their instant acceptance, the instant and total belief of the meeting members that the newcomers can make it, can stop drinking and turn their lives around. The recognition of that acceptance is one of the great spiritual experiences that one can have.

But reading the first few pages from the fifth chapter in the Big Book has another element besides the sacerdotal that makes it dangerous as a possible turn-off for the newcomer. The hopeless drunk wandering into an AA meeting has long been convinced of his hopelessness; he has tried everything, and he is sure he can neither stop drinking nor do anything else about his life. And when he hears the Big Book's statement that those who don't recover are people "constitutionally incapable of being honest with themselves," he can only feel further discouraged and hopeless because of his identification with that group. We want him to feel that the whole room believes he can make it; as a matter of fact, I believe most newcomers, given time and enough AA meetings, do make it.

Nothing stands still. AA will change, and I might as well recognize it. But I hope that such changes as occur will accentuate the free-wheeling character of AA, its friendliness, and our instant, total belief that every newcomer has what it takes, given time and enough AA meetings.

B.E., September 1974

Bye to Hi?
From Oak Lawn, Illinois:

OVER RECENT YEARS I've noticed rituals creeping into AA. This bothers me because I've never seen any of these practices approved by the group conscience in line with the Second Tradition. What usually happens is that one or more persons decide to say "Hi" or hold hands or chant, and these people begin doing so whether it is a group tradition or not.

My old home group had a tradition, voted on by the group, that we would not say "Hi," hold hands, or chant, and one of the biggest issues we had to deal with was asking visitors to honor our group traditions and refrain from ritual. Usually, the visitor would go ahead anyway and then comment that our group had something wrong with it because "everybody else does it." This group has been in existence since 1947 and has helped hundreds of suffering alcoholics recover. We made it clear that everyone was welcome at our meeting but that the group would appreciate it if all would respect our traditions. Some visitors never came back, others returned and continued to try to change our traditions by continuously saying "Hi," chanting, and so forth, attempting to void the results of our group conscience decision through peer pressure. Happily, this tactic didn't work at my home group. Unhappily, at other groups, the members wore down and gave in rather than be uncomfortable. In no case was this change the result of a group conscience decision.

This might seem very silly and childish on all sides. It's the kind of issue where I sit and inventory myself and ask why I am overreacting to such small things. Saying "Hi" seems harmless, doesn't it? After several years and several inventories, I came to the conclusion that introducing these rituals into AA is not harmless and that they may be a long-term threat to the Fellowship. I make that statement from studying the history of the Oxford Group, AA, and formal religions.

Why was the Oxford group founded? The answer is that a minister decided that a return to the early practices of Christianity was needed in order to make contact with God; he thought that the rituals that had grown up over the centuries were blocking the formation of a personal relationship with God. This is why the Oxford Group sat quietly waiting for inspiration from God to share with each other without ceremony and ritual. The Oxford Group founders saw that the focus had been taken off communion with God and placed, instead, on spending an hour or so walking through assorted ceremonies that could be performed with little or no thought. I spent years performing assorted religious rituals while thinking about what I was going to do once the ceremony was over: "Let's see, I can wash the car right after this and then pick up some milk."

To my way of thinking, ritual is what I do when I don't want to pay attention; it's a reflex. The point of every AA meeting is that I am allowed to share my experience, strength, and hope, and get to hear other members do so as well, and that's what I need to be focused on the entire time I am in the meeting. Now I spend a fair amount of time waiting for the ritual to end so I can actually listen to members share their story. At some meetings, the readings consume fifteen minutes of a one-hour meeting. I can see a day where an AA meeting will consist mainly of ritual responses and ceremony, and the sharing will be an afterthought. Where will AA be then?

I hope that the next time members say "Hi" or chant a response to a reading, they will begin to ask themselves the question, "How does this contribute to sharing what I have found in AA?"

Paul M., May 2000

Don't Just Talk About It
From Fort Collins, Colorado:

WHEN I FIRST RAN into the hand-holding ritual in the nineteen-seventies, I was visiting California. Me? Hold hands with another guy? No way. But I did, rather than be conspicuous.

You know what? I have gotten to like it. To me it is unity more than affection (though I like holding hands with women better). I can't find anything in our Traditions against it either. Are we getting too picky?

If AA is changing, perhaps one factor might be that we are losing our spirit of patience, love, and understanding. If an individual doesn't like a particular ritual, that person always has the right to decline participation. AA tells me that I should respect the rights of others.

Ray B., February 1991

Promises, Promises
From Alameda, California:

AT MANY MEETINGS I attend, the Promises are read; however, an essential idea is omitted: If we are painstaking about working Steps Eight and Nine, then "we will know a new freedom and a new happiness." Many newcomers don't read the Big Book, but they hear the Promises and wonder when they will happen to them. We need to remind ourselves that the Promises will materialize if we work the Steps.

A word about hugs. More than once I have been approached by men I don't know after a meeting, asking for a hug. When I politely decline, I have been asked, "What are you here for then?" or "You're still isolating, aren't you?" I attend AA meetings because I am an alcoholic, not to dispense—or receive—hugs.

T.W., February 1991

To Celebrate or Not to Celebrate?
From Rockaway Park, New York:

AT MY GROUP, it's customary to celebrate each anniversary with a cake, selected speakers, and a talk given by the celebrants. As I approached my first year of sobriety, I balked. I was aware that I was afraid of successes. To celebrate meant to reach a goal, and this meant I might lose.

My fellow members gave me a reason why I should celebrate: Perhaps, when I spoke at the anniversary, something I said would help someone; I could be an example for newcomers.

Last week, I decided I needed to know the difference between self-worth and ego or false pride. I asked a beautiful woman with a great deal of spirituality to help me. She had encouraged me to work the Steps when I was very new in AA, and I asked her to be my sponsor. I finished my work on the Fourth Step, then asked her to take me through my first acceptance of the Fifth Step, which was done last week and will continue in the weeks and years to come.

My Higher Power again gave me a miracle. I am now ready to really celebrate my first anniversary. I am happy and grateful, and eager to share my feelings and hopes with the people who love me. I am learning that I don't have to fear the program. There are no finished successes; there are no tops to the mountains we climb.

B.R., March 1977

Why All the Congratulations?
From New York, New York:

IT SEEMS TO ME that in the New York metropolitan area, at least, we are going badly overboard in the matter of celebrating personal anniversaries at open meetings. Of the last eight open meetings I have attended, no less than six have been "anniversaries" with, in most cases, birthday cakes with candles brought in during the meeting, singing "Happy Birthday to You," and other antics. I am somewhat loath to bring up the subject because I realize that the anniversary date—whether six months, one year, two years or longer—is a red-letter day in the life of the member. But with everyone, particularly the speakers on the program (sometimes at inordinate length), telling Joe Doaks what a grand fellow he is and what a record he has achieved, it would be too much to expect that at least some of this would not be absorbed into Joe's system—with a consequent displacement of some of his essential humility and of his hard-won knowledge that it is not Joe himself but the Higher Power who is responsible for his success. As we all know, too much "laudatory exegesis" is bad medicine for the temperamental alcoholic and, in the letdown after the celebration, too often disaster follows.

Criticism, unless it is constructive, is not helpful. I suggest, therefore, as a partial remedy, that the birthday cake and the trimmings be relegated to the coffee-and-cake period after the meeting proper is over and that the speakers on an anniversary program be requested to very strictly limit and tone down their laudatory remarks; all to the end that newcomers, as well as old-timers, will realize that the meeting is a real AA meeting and not the annual banquet of a Mutual Admiration Society.

J.A.D., February 1948

Hooray for Anniversaries
Grants Pass, Oregon:

YESTERDAY, I HAD just finished baking and decorating a large beautiful cake. I'm really up on a pink cloud and have been for days. The occasion—my husband's third AA birthday.

This is the way we celebrate here. Every birthday, whether it is the first or the twentieth, is celebrated. It is honored at the open meeting on the date closest to the anniversary. The leader of the meeting is told who has a birthday. That member is called to speak and is introduced by his sponsor if he has one. Then his wife, mother, sister, or other relative brings up a lighted cake with candles on it. The group sings "Happy Birthday." If she wants to, the wife can give a talk of two or three minutes. Some do and some don't, but those of us in Al-Anon always give a short though important one.

In our group the wife of the leader has the refreshments on the open meeting nights. We have lovely desserts with coffee after the meetings. So what if sometimes we have two or three cakes? These parties don't take up any more time than the regular meetings do and they certainly do give a lift. I get almost as much of a thrill out of other members getting a cake as I do when my husband celebrates, no matter how many candles are on it. That's because I know that the program has successfully worked for another one. Last night my husband's best friend also had a birthday cake—his second—and it was a wonderful evening.

It isn't stopping there—my husband's real birthday is Saturday. So—another party. Monday is my husband's sponsor's birthday—so Sunday I'm having a big dinner and a cake in honor of my husband, our sponsor and wife, and our best friend and wife. A three-day celebration! This happens every year. Even this three-day celebration isn't enough for me to show my husband and our friends how truly grateful I am for this wonderful AA and Al-Anon way of life.

It isn't hard for me to remember and compare how life was before my husband got AA and I joined Al-Anon. I am deeply grateful and thankful every day for this change. To our groups these celebrations are an added incentive for the newcomers to keep trying and are actual proof that the AA program can and does work. How do we know if our husbands will ever have a birthday cake with five, ten, or fifteen candles on it? If my husband does, God willing, I can tell you for sure that I will shout it from the housetops. Till then I will still get a thrill out of every one.

D.R., July 1957

Making It Real
From San Francisco, California:

NEARLY TWO YEARS in AA have made me teachable for the first time in my fifty-two years.

Among the things I've learned is that humans have always needed ritual and myth. "God as we understand Him" fills that need for myth in my life, my concept of a Higher Power to whom I can turn things over. As a third-generation atheist, "God" came hard for me but being allowed to create my own concept got me there.

Myths and rituals help us to know that there is "good orderly direction" in our lives. Holding hands and praying together reinforces our connection to each other, and to our Higher Power. The readings at the beginning of each meeting, day in and day out, create a sense of order and continuity. Ritual and myth, paradoxically, make things real for us. I believe they grow in response to the needs of the Fellowship, which are the needs of us humans trying to live a better sober life.

A.L., February 1991

Creeping Ritualism
From Portsmouth, Virginia:

I'M AN ORDAINED MINISTER with over thirty-two years of sobriety. I mention this only to say that I have some knowledge about rituals. I don't like what I refer to as creeping ritualism in the church, and I like it even less at AA meetings.

At the close of many meetings in this area, everyone joins hands, says the Lord's Prayer, and then shouts, "Keep coming back, it works if you work it." At some discussion meetings, individuals may not wish to identify themselves so they just start talking, but some rigid, ritualistic members may interrupt them, usually in a loud voice, with "What's your name?" or "Who are you?" This is a good way to assure that a shy newcomer or a timid old-timer may not return.

Not long ago I chaired a meeting during which someone shouted out two or three times, "You forgot to read the Twelve Traditions!"

Recently, I attended a large open meeting. The speaker was a minister with about fifteen years of sobriety. He suggested (no tongue in cheek) that we should sing the first verse of "Amazing Grace" before each meeting. Can you imagine the impact this would have on a newcomer? I have one friend in Kentucky with forty years of sobriety who simply leaves the room when they start to join hands.

When I came into AA in 1957, my sponsor told me that when I chaired a meeting, I could conduct it in whatever manner I choose. I'm pretty flexible and open to new ideas but I detest creeping ritualism, especially in AA.

Leo R., February 1991

The Need for Spontaneity
From Everett, Washington:

FOR MY OWN PART, I would like to see less ritual in AA. When I got sober thirteen years ago, there was only one meeting in our town. Since I didn't like to drive at night, going to other meetings in other towns was out of the question.

One night the chairman for the evening was chosen (after three or four people had declined) by saying, "Okay, the next person through the door is it." We had some fascinating meetings chaired by members of our group and a lot of visitors from other groups. No, we didn't let first-timers chair; generally we could spot them the minute they walked through the door.

We opened the meeting by reading the Preamble and "How It Works," and closed with the Lord's Prayer or the Serenity Prayer. Sometimes we had a "moment of silence" but most of the time we didn't.

I was tremendously impressed by the lack of structure and how well everything worked and everyone got along. I had belonged to ritual-type groups in the past and eventually became bored.

I find that today I have the same reactions at meetings. In our area they are all run pretty much alike, and the lack of spontaneity leaves me cold. Ritual leads to rigidity. We tend to be positive that our way is the only way, and spontaneity shows us that there are several ways to accomplish the same end.

Connie T., February 1991

Old-Fashioned AA
From Locust, New Jersey:

WITHOUT GETTING INTO a "dump session," I'd like to examine a few of the rituals found around my neck of the woods. What about choosing someone from the group to "light the candle for the still-suffering alcoholic, in hopes that he (or she) may see the light and find his way to these rooms"? What about leaving the empty chair to remind us of the suffering alcoholic who is still "out there"?

In my opinion, these cult-like rituals have no place in AA. Where are the old-timers to remind us of our roots and what meetings used to be like? They have been outnumbered by newcomers fresh from rehab who make up the majority of our members at these meetings.

The AA program has taught me that when things such as this disturb me, there is something wrong with me. The something wrong is that I'm afraid of losing the program that has kept me sane and alive for these past years. What I keep doing is finding another meeting and hoping that the "old-fashioned" style is still out there in strong supply.

S.A., February 1991

As the World Changes
From Bay City, Michigan:

THANKS TO THE AA PROGRAM I am enjoying twenty-one years of continuous sobriety. In that time I have seen many changes in meetings and have found them pleasurable. I feel a jolt of enthusiasm when we join hands and pray the Lord's Prayer. The hugs are great also. Many whom I've sponsored have commented on the warmth they felt when a member hugged them, as it had been many drunken years without a handshake or a smile from their fellow men.

My home group has an all-member meeting once a month when the group business is transacted; if a member is uncomfortable with some phase of the meeting conduct, it is addressed here. That's where the group conscience of the Second Tradition makes the decision. The Fourth Tradition tells me that if my group decides to continue these practices, so be it. If I suffer discomfort with the conduct of a group, I am free to find another home group or start one of my own with a few members who feel as I do.

As long as we don't revise the Twelve Steps, the Twelve Traditions, or the first 164 pages of our Big Book, let AA change as the world changes.

T.M., July 1991

No Less Wondrous
From Belleville, New Jersey:

WHEN I BEGAN in AA sixteen years ago, we did not hold hands to say the Lord's Prayer at the end of meetings; even the prayer was "for those who care to join us." When hand-holding began, I was standing next to a woman who, while she gripped my hand tightly in her own, noted what a spoil-sport the man next to her was, as he declined to hold her hand. I too thought the "old sourpuss" was just being obtuse. But I've changed my mind.

This business of holding hands has become one of the AA "musts," of which we say there are none, due simply to immense social pressure to conform. If you fail to put your hand into that of the next person, you are considered a grouch, if not a misanthrope. The action will be noted and taken as a negative move on your part, whether you feel comfortable doing so or not. (If you drop your hands and step back you have deprived two people of the privilege, too.) Even bringing up the subject at our group's business meeting, I was shouted down and treated as if I was against motherhood or something. Emotionalism and sentimentalism wouldn't allow an intellectual assessment. It's always harder to begin something than to end it.

My concern, however, is for the newcomer. When I was new I didn't feel particularly sociable coming to AA. I didn't want to "go to church," and had no idea what lay ahead or that I would ultimately want to be a part of it. Mainly, I didn't want to be coerced into doing anything I didn't want to. "There are no musts" was the most comforting thing I heard. The handshake at the door, shaky hands and sweaty palms notwithstanding, made no particular demand upon me, but any further physical contact (especially linked with prayer) might have been perceived as unnecessary liberty taken by "strangers." I would never have had the nerve to assert myself by not joining in, however uncomfortable it made me feel.

Rather than risking trespass on the newcomer's privacy, I would forgo this practice. We did without it for the bulk of our history. We are no less wondrous without it, and we are no more united with it.

B.F., June 1990

No Holding Hands, Please

From Southampton, New York:

HOLDING HANDS and saying the Lord's Prayer in a sing-song fashion reminds me of a maypole dance that we used to do in kindergarten. It took me many years to acquire a sensible relationship with my Higher Power, and I consider holding hands to be an invasion of my privacy. I absolutely refuse to hold hands. My God as I understand him requires me to be honest in my prayers as he does in all matters.

G.S., August 1991

Chapter 12

❖

YOUR MOVE: JANUARY & FEBRUARY 1989

Is AA Changing?

*I*n the June 1988 issue, Grapevine editors asked readers to consider the question "Is AA changing?" They noted that many of the changes are "directly related to AA's effectiveness in providing a means of recovery from alcoholism—in other words, problems stemming from the very success of AA." For most who responded, the central question was: Is AA's message of hope and recovery still being carried? Some AA members were distinctly skeptical about the answer, while others believed that, as one writer put it, "The basic concepts of love and service are alive and well." As another writer expressed it: "The principles of AA (the Steps and Traditions) are incredibly flexible, yet steadfast in their roots."

❖

Room for Growth

From Rome, New York:

I CAME INTO AA in the summer of 1971, and AA was perfect for me. I try to practice principles before personalities today, but in the beginning I needed the personalities to teach me the principles, and it seems that I met the right people at the right time.

I do think AA has changed since then, and for the better. I don't find as many dominant personalities in the meetings I attend, and since I think it best to stay a student in AA, I'm not attracted to being a dominant personality myself. A domineering old-timer can intimidate a group or individuals, and this cuts down on the freedom of expression that's vital to healthy meetings.

A newcomer can be just as helpful to me as an old-timer: my answer may come from anyone at the meeting. But if people think what they say must have someone's approval, they're not as likely to express what they really feel.

Another way that AA has changed is that we don't have as much of an opportunity to make Twelfth Step calls in a person's drinking environment. I haven't been called to go to someone's home in many years. I am on the telephone-answering list and get calls from time to time, but I think the impact of seeing the still-active alcoholic in his or her drinking environment was much stronger. It helped to keep a realistic idea of where drinking would take me, and this is most important. I need active alcoholics to remind me of how bad it really was.

Joining AA released me from my most self-destructive patterns and gave me direction in day-to-day living. AA encouraged me to continually seek growth in maturity, improve my relations with others, and seek God's will for me. One of the most rewarding things in my life is to contribute something to a meeting. Even if I don't make a big or brilliant contribution, I think it's important to give what I've got for that day.

There are no limitations on the growth I can seek and develop in trying to practice the Twelve Steps and listening at meetings. I have found a lot of help from professional sources and I can do a lot more. But my point is that there is plenty of improvement and quality I can put into my life, and the hope of doing so keeps me coming back.

C.R.

Pain Is Resistance to Change
From Royal Oak, Michigan:

OF COURSE AA IS CHANGING. Nothing is constant except change, say the sages. If the universe ever winds down into an inert, homogeneous mass, with no hills or valleys, no fire or ice, perhaps then change will cease. Until then, change is part of our existence, like it or not.

One of the many important lessons I've learned in my three short years of sobriety is that it isn't change that is painful but rather my resistance to it. Accepting change that's beyond my control, instead of trying to stand against the tide, allows me more time and energy to seek the still point within me.

Where I live, a closed meeting breaks up into several tables. Each table selects a leader and a Step to discuss, and every person at that table has an opportunity to speak. In other parts of the country, lead meetings are common, at which one person speaks and a few selected people in the group are invited to share.

I've heard people from each parochial background complain about the format of AA meetings in other areas, but the fact is, both methods are working. They are just two variations on a common theme, and people all around the world are getting and staying sober whatever format they follow.

Just as we are all different individuals, so are our groups tailored to the needs of our specific areas. Thank God we're not so rigid that we are incapable of adapting to the changing needs of our membership—we would surely destroy ourselves.

We are here, by the grace of God, to carry a message to others who want it: a message of experience, strength, and hope. It is my obligation as a recipient of this gift to make certain that the process does not end with me. As long as each of us is free to follow this path, change cannot harm us. Let us remember to "Live and Let Live."

D.C.

Inactive Newcomers
From Ridgefield Park, New Jersey:

YES, AA IS CHANGING, and here is my thinking. Before I start, I'd like to say that I've been "actively" sober for close to ten years.

1) There is no such thing as a sponsor anymore. Newcomers won't

use the phone at all—only if, and when, they're in trouble. Then we're supposed to be at their beck and call. They want instant success—but don't want to work at it.

2) There is no—repeat no—involvement in groups. You have to beg to find someone to make the coffee, buy the cake, go on commitments. The newer people don't want to do it. It is the old-timers who are behind the coffee pots, setting up and cleaning up, taking the commitments. And if you're not there to do the above-mentioned things, it's as if you've committed a crime. I got it recently when I asked someone to go to a meeting to book incoming speakers from other groups and the reply was, "I went twice already." Just to set the record straight, I've been doing all of these for years, most of the time by myself.

3) The newer people are concerned only with seeing their names on the cake for their ninety- day and subsequent anniversaries. In the meantime, where are they? Perhaps someone gave them a subscription to *TV Guide* for their ninety-day anniversary.

4) Where is gratitude? In the dictionary?

AA has given me more than I ever wanted in my life. And what I have now, I got from people passing it down to me and showing me a way to live—a day at a time. I wouldn't trade this Fellowship for all the money in the world. My life is in order. Thanks are due to the Fellowship, my Higher Power (whom I choose to call God), and the founders of AA for giving me a place to recover.

M.M.

Love and Patience
From Providence, Rhode Island:

I CAME INTO THIS FELLOWSHIP in October 1975 and got sober in January 1976. I was approaching my twenty-fifth birthday, had shoulder-length hair (I now have no hair on top), had patches on my blue jeans and holes in my boots. I shook, I was scared, and I had a tremendous amount of anger inside of me. I had also been a heroin addict, although I was pretty much off heroin three years before I came into AA. Alcohol, for the final three years of my thirteen years of alcoholism and drug addiction, brought me to my knees. I had hit rock bottom.

When I first arrived, some people didn't approve of the way I looked. Nor did they think I had the right to be here because of my age and my drug history. I was later told that people were taking bets that I wasn't ready for this program. (This is a practice I don't approve of, but I've done the same to others.)

What is this all leading up to? Because of the love of the people in AA who encouraged me in my early sobriety, and who continue to do so today, I was able to go to young people's conferences in Rhode Island and Canada, as well as AA conventions and roundups. When I was seven months sober, I was fortunate to be involved in starting a young people's group in my area, a group that is still meeting today. I serve as DCM for my district. I am now married to a woman in the Fellowship, and we have two beautiful AA babies.

I can't help but wonder what my life would be like if it weren't for the love and patience of those old-timers and other members who told me that if I was having a problem with alcohol, I was in the right place. I can't help but ask myself, "Are these problems we face today in AA any different from the problems faced by the early members of AA?" What happened when the first woman or the first drug addict or the first gay person came to an AA meeting?

The only requirement for AA membership is a desire to stop drinking. It doesn't matter whether we are dually-addicted or sent by the courts or come from a treatment center. None of use came here out of virtue. When most of us arrived, we felt we were being sentenced. I have yet to see too many people stick around too long if they really don't have a problem with alcohol.

I think we can overcome the problems that face AA today through our ability to apply the suggestions of the Twelve Steps and Twelve Traditions in our lives. I truly believe what I've heard said: that our problems don't come from outside the Fellowship but from the way we deal with issues inside it. So I hope we will use love, patience, and tolerance with our fellow alcoholics and guide them along the path of sobriety.

B.R.

Lack of Power
From Oak Lawn, Illinois:

MY QUESTION IS: "How have AA meetings changed?" My answer: In the nineteen years I've been an active member of AA, I've seen many AA meetings deteriorate into nothing more than whiner-and-moaner sessions or massive complaint meetings with little or no mention of the foundation of the AA program that is so beautifully expressed in the Big Book.

Far too many AA members carry into a meeting a problem that should be discussed first with a sponsor or held for discussion with several AA friends at "the meeting after the meeting."

When I was introduced to AA in 1969, meetings were for discussion of the Steps. Problems were to be discussed only with AA solutions in mind and not as a forum for the most elaborate complaint of the day. Today, AA meetings are being diluted with subjects that aren't even related to alcoholism. Far too many members are using a broken shoelace as an excuse for indulging their own self-centered life experiences.

Finally, never in my time in AA has the saying "If you want to hide something from an alcoholic, put it in the Big Book" been more appropriate.

Maybe it's time to turn AA meetings into AA meetings and not into self-indulgent, petty gripe sessions where nothing is heard about using the basics of our God-inspired Twelve Step program of recovery.

The Big Book tells me that "lack of power was our dilemma." Let's get back to those teachings at meetings and leave the whiners and moaners to see the fallacy of their self-pity and self-centered discussions.

B.C.

Keeping It Simple
From Akron, Ohio:

I SUPPOSE SINCE AA is growing, it is also changing, and this is good because it means more people are afforded the opportunity of recovery. But we have to continue to "Keep It Simple" and stick with the basics.

In our area, a variety of new for-profit programs have developed, some of which are spin-offs of our Twelve Step program. There are also new treatment centers for problems other than alcoholism and, in some cases, new philosophies.

I am distressed that some practices of these outside programs have been sneaking into local AA meetings. I have even seen what I would observe as recruitment for non-AA meetings. Well-meaning counselors who may not be aware of the tremendous personal growth opportunities provided by AA and the Twelve Steps are referring alcoholics to treatment at treatment centers that have a different focus.

Our Tradition Six clearly states that we have "no opinion on outside issues" and, as the Preamble says, we are "not allied with any sect, denomination, politics, organization or institution." So I take no issue with such centers—just as I take no issue with a person's religion. I do take issue with outside programs being brought into AA meetings or persons recruiting for other programs while in AA meetings. Those of us who have been around a while must tell such individuals, "We appreciate your point of view but, because of our Traditions, we would ask that you disseminate your information outside of this meeting place" or simply ask the individuals to stay on the AA topics or subjects of the meeting.

During my own recovery, there have been misspent times when I have gone "shopping" for other solutions to my alcoholism or have tried to find ways to blame relatives or friends or institutions for my problems. This seems common among alcoholics.

With a spirit of love and tolerance, the program must protect itself. It has been so important to my own recovery to learn—and relearn—the principles of Alcoholics Anonymous. How dear our familiar slogan is: "Keep It Simple"!

J.B.

No More Plastic Clones
From Grants, New Mexico:

TEN OR TWELVE YEARS AGO, a surge of baby-boomers moved into the Colorado Springs area, changing both the community and AA. Traditions and gentleness, AA and otherwise, seemed to be on the way out. In the face of these changes, my husband and I moved to a small northern New Mexico community about a year ago. We've been delightedly grinning at each other ever since.

Not once in this past year have we heard the words "relationship" or "commitment" or any other "in" words we were hearing from the baby-boomers back in Colorado. What few swear words heard are said for emphasis not for lack of vocabulary. Not one person has blathered endlessly about the sins, rituals, myths or hair shirts of the healthy religion at the meetings here. There is no time nor inclination for such sophistry.

The average age is about the same here. Anglo, Indian, and His-panic come to our two meetings a week through the courts and treatment centers and family pressure, just like up north. Otherwise, it's like wiping that ten years of change off the face of our AA expe-rience. There is warmth and love here, and each person digs deep inside for the words and wisdom and experience to convey AA prin-ciples. Many cannot afford to come to both meetings and so we try to give each other enough love and support to last until we can meet again. There is no room for bickering, and nobody wants to waste a minute of the meeting.

These people are like the ones we knew years ago: basically gen-tle, full of humor and innate good manners. They are real alcoholics, all right. They are also real people—individuals—not abrasive, not plastic clones like those we encountered in the changing urban meetings.

We're grateful to our Higher Power for the reprieve, however long it may last.

M.R.

Many Paths
From Rochester, New York:

THE QUESTION "IS AA CHANGING?" deserves a thoughtful response. I think one of the issues that needs to be addressed is the difference in the needs of newcomers who come in by different routes—in partic-ular those who come in "off the street" (as I did) and those who come in having sobered up in detoxes and rehabs. I've often felt disadvan-taged because I knew practically nothing about AA (or alcoholism) when I came into it; or, to be more accurate, I had a lot of stereotyped notions and a little bit of what turned out to be misinformation. Fellow newcomers who came from detoxes and rehabs seemed to have a good deal of information and understanding that I didn't have. In addition, they'd been "dry" a little while; I "dried out" in AA.

To compound the problem, there seemed to be a common assump-tion that everybody was at the same level (which certainly wasn't true), and that if we needed to know something we'd ask. Trouble was, I didn't know the questions! I was so confused, so full of guilt and shame, that I couldn't look anybody in the eye (much less say "alcoholic" out loud); I couldn't make sense out of "high bottom/ low bottom," "pink cloud," "qualify," *et cetera*; and I was just generally miserable (ask any member of my home group—they remember it well!).

I finally did "come to," and I don't in any way resent those who come to AA in a more teachable condition, though I have to admit that I sometimes envy them.

The solution? I'd say more emphasis on beginner meetings. (I'd been around almost six months before I found out there was such a thing.) Above all, I think it's important to remember that there are many ways that newcomers get to AA; the important thing is that we get here at all, and that we stay long enough to begin to get the message. I did. And I will be eternally grateful.

Anonymous

The Age of Indifference?
From Effingham, Illinois:

IS AA CHANGING? Yes, I really think it is—and not for the better. My home group has changed in the last twelve years since I came into AA. We are getting quite a few "young-in-years" dual addicts. I would say about two-thirds of these young people have been to a detox/treatment center and have not learned or tried to adhere to the principles of Alcoholics Anonymous that we learned from the older members when I entered the doors of AA.

I sponsor some of these young dual addicts and so far I cannot seem to convince them of the importance of taking their Fourth and Fifth Steps. There is much indifference concerning our AA program and how we work it versus how they want to work it.

Our AA program is a very sound program and was inspired by God, and we members must keep it that way. But I have a serious question. What do we do as faithful and active members when newcomers and dual addicts say "I am an addict," or "I am a user"? If they are both addicts and alcoholics, they refer to being an addict first. They usually start telling their experiences in "using" rather than their uses of alcohol.

V.B.

Don't Know
From Troy, New York:

I BELIEVE THE WISEST of people often say "I don't know." Those three words are my immediate response to the question, "Is AA changing?"

What I do know is that I once read an article in the Grapevine depicting the demise of someone's home group, and I was frightened by the idea that the Fellowship could fall apart. My fear was allayed when a friend said, "As long as we have the Steps, we have the program of Alcoholics Anonymous."

But I see many people who are afflicted by the fear that AA might break down—a fear of change that manifests itself as a fear of the people and practices that are considered nontraditional in the Fellowship.

Are these unusual people and practices changing AA? I don't know, but I do know that the Third and Twelfth Steps and the Second Tradition have shown themselves to be worthy of my trust. So long as I work the Third Step, I will not be led too far away from the Fellowship. And if I try to practice the principles of AA in all my affairs then I carry the program with me even when I am alone. Likewise, so long as we all, as group members and individuals, try to work the Second Tradition, then the Fellowship will not be led too far away from me. Because I have seen this in the Steps and the Second Tradition, one more of my fears has been replaced by faith. I need not shudder or drive myself neurotic with the anxiety that I shall be left alone feeling helpless and abandoned the way I felt just before I came into AA. Today I love and I feel that I am loved.

My name is Timothy, I'm an alcoholic, and I participate in a beautiful Fellowship. These truths are not likely to change soon; in fact, if I work this program today and continue to do so one day at a time, these truths probably won't ever change.

T.M.

Turning Over in Their Graves
From Redwood Estates, California:

WHATEVER HAPPENED to the good old days of AA? Whatever happened to talking about the disease and sharing our experience, strength, and hope? Whatever happened to "We're only one drink away from a drunk," "It's the first drink that gets us drunk," and "Live and Let Live"?

I go to meetings and all I seem to hear is transforming jargon.

It's currently very fashionable to be in AA, our meetings are full of court referrals, more and more special interest groups are forming, and meetings are larger, with fancier and fancier "munchies" on smart trays. Our founders must be turning over in their graves with all that has been added to the simple, down-to-earth, one-drunk-talking-to-another program they so carefully put together many years ago. I wish I knew the answer and could put it all back the way it was twelve years ago, but I know that is impossible.

All I know is that today I'm not willing to turn my will and my life over to the care of alcohol.

B.H.

A Haven Free of Dogma
From Mill Valley, California:

THE SUBSTANCE OF THIS letter is to discuss "the point of no return," and whether AA has passed it with regard to a certain popular practice, namely that of introducing oneself, "My name is XYZ, and I'm an alcoholic." It seems to have acquired the status of an institutional rite or ceremony whereby it has become commonplace in my community for a member to be shouted down by the group and not permitted to speak until personal identification is satisfied—in the prescribed manner—each time the member would like to speak. I'll bet there are many members who don't realize that it was not always so.

Moved by a vague but irrepressible conviction that a ritual tends to consume its observer, I would rather return to the days when an AA meeting was a comfortable refuge, a haven free of dogma, free of rites and ceremonies; but I'm afraid we have passed the point of no return.

R.C.

Our Achilles' Heel
From Santa Rosa, California:

I CAME TO AA three years ago in a small community in Oregon and am just now feeling comfortable after a year in this much, much larger fellowship in Santa Rosa. I'm thirty-eight, a woman, a "pure" alcoholic, and I have never been through a treatment program.

I believe the principles of AA (the Steps and Traditions) are incredibly flexible, yet steadfast in their roots. I believe that debating, arguing, and discussing things a hundred times over is what we are all about. And I think it is truly amazing how often when things seem just about to fall apart, someone will remind us of a basic truth about those principles that have saved so many lives.

I believe that courts and rehabs and treatment counselors need to know more about us in even the simplest of terms, i.e., the difference between open and closed meetings and that the dually-addicted need to be sent to programs designed to address their "drug of choice."

I believe we need more "education" meetings, open meetings that cover what we are and are not. We need a place where the newcomer can ask questions and get answers for anything from "Who's God?" to "Where's the bathroom?"

Whether it's a judge or a rehab program that gets a person to our doors doesn't really matter. It's whether AA can continue to offer the quality of clear-headed, non-resentful sobriety that counts.

I've heard people introduce themselves as "addicts" or "addict/alcoholics" at some of our meetings, and I wonder, Did anyone tell those people or their rehab counselors there are meetings and even entire programs especially designed for the problems of drug addiction? And then I also wonder what I am doing to alleviate my own nefarious slide into resentment, for it is resentment which is the AA member's Achilles' heel.

C.Z.

Our Attitude Must Change
From Toronto, Ontario:

ALCOHOLICS ANONYMOUS must change in order to survive. The change must come in the attitudes of some who follow our Twelve Step program of recovery. It is not the Steps, Traditions, or principles that require fine-tuning. Our problem lies in our refusal to adapt to the changing face of addiction. No longer will the "pure" alcoholics be the dominant member of this Fellowship. Increasingly we are seeing people come to this program who are poly-addicted—addicted to more than one substance. We must not stray from our primary purpose of helping the alcoholic who still suffers, but our attitude must change toward those who are cross-addicted.

Are those of us who are "pure" alcoholics somehow better than those who are addicted to other substances? Hardly. Yet one would think so by the reaction of some members. Our attitude must change from that of superiority to compassion.

AA represents hope to countless people. They come to us in sickness and fear, many testing the waters of our port in the storm. If they're in the wrong place, then we have a responsibility to welcome them and then direct them to the help they need. We must never lose sight of the fact that we are dealing with people's lives. Surely those of us who have suffered the pain of disease can respond to the pain of another with compassion rather than anger.

In the last analysis, as a recovering alcoholic I need only have two concerns. The first is to maintain my sobriety on a daily basis and to practice the program of AA one day at a time. The second is to ensure that what was here yesterday will be here tomorrow for the next alcoholic who walks through the doors of this Fellowship. And for that I am responsible.

T.C.

Practicing Practice
From San Diego, California:

I'M A PRODUCT of a Navy treatment facility. I didn't ask to go to treatment, and I didn't want to go to AA meetings, but my career was on the line and I did as I was told.

I knew I drank a lot but not once during the six weeks I was in treatment did it occur to me that I might be an alcoholic—most of what I heard discussed as symptoms of alcoholism had been facts of my life long before I picked up my first drink.

I'm convinced today, as I look back, that drinking was not the primary symptom of my disease. I'm also convinced that sustained abstinence from alcohol is not the primary symptom of my recovery, either. My abuse of alcohol was the exterior manifestation of a disease much more complex and consuming than simple drunkenness, and similarly, my abstinence is the exterior manifestation of a wellness much more rewarding than simple sobriety. The most convincing evidence I have today that I'm an alcoholic is not how much or how long I drank, nor how drunk I got; the most convincing evidence I have is that Alcoholics Anonymous is working for me.

I think the application of AA's principles and the environment in which they are practiced is changing because the human race, including alcoholics, is changing. As the human race matures and becomes more complex and subtle, so must alcoholism change its tactics and become even more "cunning, baffling, and powerful" in response.

I am infinitely grateful that AA, while founded in the Steps, Traditions, and Concepts that often seem sacred and unreproachable, was flexible enough to meet the changing nature of my disease and make possible a way of life I didn't dare dream was available to someone like me, a life rooted in love and spiritual growth.

For me to claim that whatever changes are occurring in AA are either "better" or "worse" is to question the wisdom of the collective conscience of AA, or, according to our Second Tradition, a loving God.

I've had both newcomers and old-timers alike redirect me in those times when I've veered off course. And the only one who I have to see gets to a meeting, and pays attention while he's there, is me.

I believe the most important word in AA is "practice." Our Twelfth Step says we must "practice these principles in all our affairs." For me that means all my affairs—even when there's nobody around to see me doing it. And it means action. I can talk about practice for the rest of my life, but if I don't practice practice, nothing changes.

M.W.

Diamond in the Rough
From Wilkins Township, Pennsylvania:

ALCOHOLICS ANONYMOUS has been changing since its very beginning. For example, Bill and Bob changed from self-centered individuals into men who could feel the pain of others and participate in life.

I am changing, and there are more like me starting this process every day, so Alcoholics Anonymous must be changing. Yet the process and direction in which we are moving is the same. The more it changes, the more it stays the same.

From time to time, I attend a Big Book discussion meeting, and there are always parts of the first five chapters that seem new to me. This Fellowship is like a diamond whose message flashes toward me every time I hold it up to the light and turn it around.

B.H.

Opening Doors and Hearts
From Huntsville, Alabama:

THERE IS REALLY NOTHING permanent except change.

In 1964, when I first entered the Fellowship, my sponsor, who was an old-timer at that point, said that when he came into AA, if you had a pair of shoes that matched and a wristwatch, they told you to go back out, you hadn't reached your bottom yet. Another man who had about eighteen years at the time said that if you still had a job, you weren't ready for AA.

When I came into AA the vast majority of members were still men. I was thirty-seven years old and considered young for getting sober. And there was still a real stigma connected with being in AA.

But look at the changing membership in AA today: the vast number of women — many of them young women. Look at those who still have their marriages, their families, their jobs. Although some of us coming into AA back in the nineteen-sixties had used drugs such as tranquilizers, they were a small part of our addiction. Today drugs and alcohol often go hand in hand.

Thank God AA has changed, that we have opened our doors and hearts to women, that we are able to help those newcomers now flooding to AA to change their lives without going through the suffering that we had to years back.

Yes, there is nothing permanent but change in anything that survives, and AA is not only surviving but is flourishing, thanks to God and all those who keep coming in.

R.B.

Looking for Answers
From Little Rock, Arkansas:

THE MAJOR CHANGE I've noticed over the past nine years is the large number of drug addicts coming to our meetings. Last week I attended a meeting of about twenty-five people, mostly under forty years old, and everyone (except me) introduced themselves as "an alcoholic and an addict." Two stated that they were simply "addicts."

I realize that drug addicts must find help for their problems, but I am uncomfortable sharing my experiences with someone who is not an alcoholic.

At sixty-five years of age, I know there is a generation gap. But how do I resolve my feelings?

S.C.

Serious Dependency
From Pacific Grove, California:

I CAME TO AA almost six years ago. At the time, I was living in California and was twelfth-stepped into the AA Fellowship by a group of people whom today I count among my closest friends.

My entry into AA was marked by periods of depression, uncertainty, and cynicism, but through the love of these people I was able to lessen the pain and begin living a life of happiness and fulfillment I had not known was possible. This new life did not cost me a nickel. It was only later that I discovered these good people were helping me not only to fulfill some noble, altruistic goal, but that they were also acting in a selfish way to keep themselves sober by practicing the Twelfth Step, which states: "Having had a spiritual awakening as the result of these Steps, we tried to carry the message to alcoholics, and to practice these principles in all our affairs."

About a year ago, my job took me to an area where Twelfth Step work was much less common. The reason for this seemed to be the large number of treatment centers and programs that were there. The treatment centers were charging large sums of money to teach people how to go to AA meetings. This bothered me because, as I said, I got it for free. But the more serious problem was the growing dependency of AA members on treatment centers to do the Twelfth Step work that helps keep us sober. So the question I'd like to pose is: Who's carrying the message these days, AA or Sunnybrook Farms?

B.L.

Blessings Abound
From Islip Terrace, New York:

I CAME INTO AA in 1967 from the Central Islip State Hospital program. I was twenty-six years old, had been on the Bowery, in hospitals, and in jails. I had pneumonia, had lost my equilibrium, and was getting stomped on the streets.

I called the only person who would talk to me, a Catholic priest. He said, "Mike, what do I have to do—cut your throat to stop you from drinking?" I said, "Father, I'll do anything." He took me to Central Islip.

Part of the hospital program at that time was to attend outside AA meetings. We all wore grey shirts with CISH stamped onto the back. Most people at the meetings remained neutral to us, but some came up and tried to be friendly. Some of them would yell, "These hospital people drink the coffee, eat the cake, and don't contribute to the group. We'll go broke." But these people changed as more and more "hospital people" stayed sober, joined groups, and became active.

Today we are blessed with thousands of meetings in hospitals, prisons, and treatment facilities. There are thousands of young people now in AA who came in through institutions and job-related programs. And many of these programs were fought for and started by the hard-core critics who at one time said the "hospital people" contributed nothing to the group.

When I got out of the hospital and joined the Islip Group, there were only two other young guys in AA in this area. Some of the old-timers said to me "I spilled more than you drank," and that I didn't have too much of a chance to stay sober. But a couple of people who were the coffee makers, the clean-up people—the backbone of the group—reached out. They gave me a will to live and a faith to live by. And as I grew in AA, the critics became my best friends.

Last April, I celebrated my twenty-first anniversary, and I took a look at AA today. I see a lot of people who still have their families, their houses, their jobs. These people may never have to know the pain of the streets.

I also see lots of young people in AA. These young people have an honesty and openness that I admire. Some have a dual addiction problem (alcohol and narcotics) just as many years ago some members had a dual addiction problem (alcohol and gambling, or alcohol and pills, for example). And yet, over the years I've found that if a person is an alcoholic with other problems and he remains sober in AA, the other problems subside. If the person is not an alcoholic, however, we can't help with his other problems.

Today, at forty-seven years of age, I see AA as being stronger than ever. I see a more open love in the Fellowship and the free extending of hope. I see changes in AA, but changes for the good. The basic concepts of love and service are alive and well.

M.O.

Wearing Out the Hammer
From Mexico:

AFTER THIRTY-FOUR YEARS in the AA way of life—the last twenty-seven sober—I've come to see what AA is all about: my sobriety! Put together by alcoholics, for alcoholics, and made up of alcoholics, AA is not bound by complicated and stringent rules. It is a loosely knit spiritual fellowship.

I've grown up in AA. I've also grown old. I have found great joy, and had that joy turn into terrible sorrow, but I endure. What else can I do?

Many of the original AAs, if still alive, would be in their nineties, some over 100 years old. They were born into and lived in a totally different world, yet the basic insecurities common to mankind—to say nothing of all the rest of the ills of human life—were the same. The last 5,000 years and the next 5,000 years will be no different in my view.

The anvil wears out the hammer: the anvil of AA truth and the hammer of dissension. AA as we know it may not survive 100 years more, but I believe its basic form and truths will be alive and well, even after AA is gone.

O.E.

Chapter 13

❖

FLASHES OF SANITY

Experiencing Moments of Insight

A story in the Third Edition of the Big Book ("Rum, Rebellion, and Radio") describes how one man came out of a drunken stupor to experience "a flash of sanity" when he suddenly knew he had to stop drinking.

In sobriety, these flashes of sanity continue. We experience moments of insight, understanding, humor, and grace — gifts that we can carry forward into our lives. In the letters that follow, AA members share their moments with the rest of us.

❖

Miraculous Experience
From Toledo, Ohio:

ABOUT FIVE YEARS AGO, I had probably the most miraculous experience of my life. For a long time I couldn't talk about it when I led a meeting. I was afraid it would sound incredible or invented.

At the time, I was a secretary for the AA central office and had been sober about eight months. This particular afternoon my morale was very low, brought about by an upset which had plunged me into dire, black, unhealthy thinking. Those bad thoughts soon tied in with "What's the use" and "Maybe one or two martinis." They persisted to a point where nothing mattered—except to go out and get "a couple."

One person was sitting in the outer room. I was very quiet. My thoughts raced in sly scheming. I locked up the cash box, asked the man if he could tend my office for an hour or so (!), got on my coat, and took three steps toward the door when the phone rang. I walked back to answer it, irritated by the interruption. It was just a call for information about meeting hours. I hung up but I didn't get up.

I saw something which made me sit still . . . very still.

I saw a scale, a large, old-fashioned scale, the kind country storekeepers use, with a five-pound weight on one platform balancing a sack of goods like sugar or flour on the other. Only I didn't see sugar nor the weight.

I saw five little packages done in tissue paper, tied with a ribbon and neatly labeled: Health, Husband, Home, Happiness, and Job.

On the other platform, perfectly balancing the little packages, was one martini with an olive shimmering in the bottom of the glass.

The apparition stayed in front of me. I looked at it long and deeply.

The significance began to make itself felt. For a woman who had been a nonbeliever, I knew I could no longer question the real, tangible presence of a Higher Power. My head went down on my desk, and I cried and shook, but I repeated over and over, "Thank you God."

That was the turning point for me. From that time on, the Twelve Steps made sense, and I accepted them without question. Many, many times every day, I contact my particular loving, forgiving Higher Power. I sincerely try to accept his plan for me and ask for guidance.

Anytime the thoughts of a drink flash through my mind, I ask myself if I want the result. And I bring back the startlingly clear picture of the country scales, never failing to say, "Thank you, God."

D.V.A., October 1952

A Way To Measure Serenity
From Conjilon, New Mexico:

EARLY IN MY SOBRIETY, I got angry at my wife and stormed out of the house. Instead of going to a bar, I went to the AA clubhouse where I found my sponsor sitting at a table. I turned the air blue with profanity and told him, "That !#$*! tried to tell me how to hang a curtain rod."

He began to laugh and that made me madder. When I finally calmed down and asked him what was so $%#!* funny, he looked at me and said, "Bill, we are only as big as the smallest thing that makes us angry."

That was over fifteen years ago, and when I begin to get angry, I still ask myself, "How big am I?" Sometimes I can be pretty small.

Bill W., August 1998

A Different Prayer for Different Results
From De Beque, Colorado:

MY PRAYER USED TO BE, "Lord, give me strength and courage and fortitude; please give me peace of mind and serenity." Always I asked for something, ending with the usual thanks for all my blessings (which sometimes was a bit feeble). I was given some of the things I asked for; that is, I got them eventually, after I had prayed and prayed. Now and then my pleas were answered promptly, usually in cases of great stress.

One day I got to wondering if the affirmative approach wouldn't bring better results. After all, he who cares for the sparrows surely knows our needs, even before we ask. And so, I began praying in a slightly different way. Instead of asking, I would say, "God, you are giving me strength and courage and fortitude; you are giving me serenity and peace of mind. Thank you, God, for all this and for many blessings."

Since then, my prayers have been answered much more quickly; often I have received courage and peace of mind immediately. Whenever my prayers go unanswered, I know I have prayed amiss, and that God in his wisdom is giving me what is best for me. So I then say, "Thy will be done, not mine."

W.F., December 1955

Southern Hospitality
From New York, New York:

I WAS SCHEDULED to fly to Tampa, Florida. Because of a local storm, we took off three hours late and arrived at Tampa at two in the morning. My frustration hit an all-time high when I was informed that my hotel reservation had been made for the following night. After a few minutes of negotiation, the hotel arranged for me to stay in a nearby motel.

It was now 2:45 A.M., and the terminal was deserted. I walked out the door and got a sudden chill. Coming directly toward me were two county troopers. Having no experience at being a lonely Yankee in a Southern town, I was sure that I was going to get busted for loitering in the airport.

One trooper stopped at a drinking fountain. The other stopped three feet in front of me and said, "You're from New York, aren't you?" I thought he knew that since the New York plane was the last one in. "And," he continued, "you're a friend of Bill W.'s."

I almost fainted with relief when I realized that AA had reached out to me when I was a thousand miles from home, hungry, angry, lonely, and tired.

The trooper was a man named Chuck, formerly of New York, and he had recognized me as a speaker he'd heard at an AA meeting two years previously.

This certainly is a strong argument in favor of carrying the message and continuing AA activity.

G.W., December 1976

Looks Can Be Deceiving
From Rota, Spain:

RECENTLY SOME MEN came to my house to do some heavy yard work, and in doing so, they pruned the bushes separating my neighbor's yard from mine. As they led me outside to show me their accomplishment, it took all my feeble acting ability to hide my shock and disappointment. On the eight bushes, I could not find more than three leaves. I like my neighbors, but I truly appreciated the privacy the bushes offered; and when the harsh Levante winds rushed in from the desert, their value as a windbreak would be greatly missed. To all appearances, the bushes were dead.

When the first new leaves began to appear, I was delighted, but there were still many dead branches and I knew I had to prune them. For several weeks, every glimpse of the bushes was a painful reminder of the job that had to be done; and the guilt over my procrastination grew.

Finally I found the time for the task, and I was thankful for the many excuses I'd invented for putting off the job. Many of the branches that had seemed lifeless a few weeks before had now started to bud. A few weeks ago, I couldn't have told death from life, or differentiated between the worthwhile and the unproductive.

Perhaps I won't be so anxious to solve all my problems today. Blindly rushing in to hack away at character defects will not speed recovery and may actually slow it down. My Higher Power knows the right time to reveal the life-producing parts of me, and if I have patience, I will know clearly what parts need to be cut away. Not long ago, my life looked like dead sticks. Now, in those branches that carry life, buds are starting to appear. I can rejoice in the new life, and in the newfound wisdom to wait for it.

K.H., January 1991

Depends on Your Point of View
From Hollywood, Florida:

ONE MEETING I ENJOY a lot is an "Ask-It Basket" meeting where written questions are put in a basket as it's passed around the room. One night the chairman read, "What is the difference between shortcomings and defects of character?"

After a moment of thought, I raised my hand and said, "I have shortcomings; everyone else has defects of character."

Bill K., January 1995

Thankful
From Cumberland, England:

IT RECENTLY OCCURRED to me that, of all the living creatures on this earth, man is the only one who prays or has a need to. Prayer need not be a formalized routine of words or a childish request for favors; nor is it a refuge for weaklings. Prayer is a mature activity which enables us to achieve complete harmony of mind, body, and spirit; it is a means of harnessing our finite energy to the infinite energy of God.

Prayer has become a habit with me. Anytime is the time for prayer: in the street, in the factory, sitting still, walking about, or actively engaged upon some task. I must always bear in mind that, like a good parent, God often says no. And the simplest prayer is "God, thank you, thank you." I have so much to be thankful for, and sobriety tops the list.

G.H., March 1967

The Gift of Hearing
From Green Valley, Arizona:

I AM A 74-YEAR-OLD male AA with twenty-eight years of as active a sobriety as I'm capable of handling. During the course of a regular check-up with my internist (a woman doctor and a skillful diagnostician), my health was as good as it could be. My only complaint was a feeling of sadness—not for myself, but for the loss of so many older AA friends.

My doctor listened patiently and said, "Have you ever heard of a Higher Power?" We put away the medical agenda and started another kind of conversation.

During the course of our discussion, it occurred to me that I had forgotten two important things. First, our Fellowship has proven that "this too shall pass." And second, when all my tools have been exhausted, sometimes I just have to sit still and hurt, and have the patience to wait for it to pass.

My doctor admitted that she too has a limited capacity with her medical knowledge, and sometimes has to turn it over. I am grateful that there are nonalcoholics with this gift of hearing.

E. B., November 1992

Aren't People Funny?
From New York, New York:

IF YOU TELL A PERSON that there are 270,678,934,341 stars in the universe, he'll believe you. But if you tell an alcoholic to stay away from "that first drink," he has to make a personal investigation.

Anonymous, June 1950

A Full Meal
From Kanata, Ontario:

I REMEMBER WHEN I bought my first Big Book, I was told by an old-timer that "meetings are the icing on the cake, but the Big Book is the meat in the sandwich." The AAs who were standing around the literature table that night all nodded knowingly at this metaphor. I realize now just how true those words are.

Gary S., October 1994

Wx'rx All Hxrx!
From Granite Falls, Minnesota:

XVXN THOUGH MY TYPXWRITXR is an old modxl, it works quitx wxll xxcxpt for onx of thx kxys. I'vx wishxd many timxs that it workxd pxrfxctly. It is trux that thxrx arx forty-six kxys that function wxll xnough, but just onx kxy not working makxs thx diffxrxncx.

Somxtimxs it sxxms to mx that our AA program is somxwhat likx my typxwritxr . . . not all thx kxy pxoplx arx working propxrly.

You may say to yoursxlf, "Wxll, I am only onx pxrson. What if I miss a mxxting or two? I won't makx or brxak thx program." But it doxs makx a diffxrxncx bxcausx thx AA program, to bx xffxctivx, nxxds thx activx participation of xvxry mxmbxr.

So thx nxxt timx you think you arx only onx pxrson and that your xfforts arx not nxxdxd, rxmxmbxr my typxwritxr and say to yoursxlf, "I am a kxy pxrson in our AA program, and I am nxxdxd vxry much."

E.H.B., May 1957

Legal Age for Alcoholism
From St. Catharines, Ontario:

THE FIRST TIME I HEARD of AA was in the compound at a state prison. I overheard two fellows talking about it, and I asked them questions. They told me there were weekly AA meetings inside, and I could easily get permission from the warden to attend.

The warden called me into his office when he got my request. He glared at me suspiciously and said, "How old are you?"

I knew he knew, but I said, "Eighteen."

"You're not even old enough to buy a drink legally," he said. "You couldn't possibly be an alcoholic. I can't give you permission to go to those meetings."

Naturally I flared with resentment. The more I brooded over that conversation, and the more I looked at my record, proving to the warden in my mind that I was an alky, the more I proved it to myself!

My two fellow inmate sponsors kept talking to me, and as soon as I got out of prison, I joined AA—"legally." That warden packed quite a message.

Anonymous, February 1963

CARD Tricks
From Kittery, Maine:

ON BAD DAYS I come home and just stew. My sponsor has told me all the things to do to stay sober at such times, but I keep forgetting a few. Then I remembered a trick from my college days—using a memory aid. So, CARDS has become my recipe for sobriety: Call your sponsor, Ask for help from your Higher Power, Read the Big Book, Do the Twelve Steps, Stay active in your group.

B.P., September 1993

In the Line
From Tujunga, California:

A FRIEND OF MINE told me about going to see the Statue of Liberty on a field trip with his grammar school class. He said that as they walked up the long spiral staircase, they all held hands in a line. He couldn't see the person at the beginning or the end of the line, but he felt safe. He knew he was connected to the rest of his schoolmates. That's the way it is in AA. We can't see the people at the beginning of the line or the end of the line. But we know they're there—and we know we're safe.

Doug R., December 1997

Good Luck!
From Dallas, Texas:

I BELIEVE IN WISHING a man good luck. I believe in hoping for good things, for anybody, anywhere, anytime. I believe in asking for things. If anything's worth asking for once, it's worth asking for again. On these grounds, I ask that God grant you the grace and the common sense to see yourself as he sees you, that you may better know yourself and his will, and be enabled to carry it out in your daily life. I ask that he carry on, in you and through you, the gifts of his grace, and of his good give you plenty. I ask that his favors reward you, his spirit guide you, his power protect you.

Now send one up for me. Just a little quickie.

Anonymous, August 1955

The Laugh's on Me
From Elbur, Illinois:

I WAS HAVING A PROBLEM at work: I was becoming increasingly frustrated by people who were making unfair demands upon my time and attention. But I couldn't find a way to deal with it. One morning, I began my morning prayers and got to the line from the Seventh Step prayer that says, "I pray that you remove every single defect of character which stands in the way of my usefulness to you and my fellows." But out of my mouth instead came these words: "I pray that you remove every single defective character who stands in my way!"

Hearing my own true thoughts so bluntly announced in this way—and in the middle of a prayer, no less—made me suddenly laugh aloud. It relieved all the tension I'd allowed to build inside me. This slip of the tongue was a gift from my Higher Power, showing me gently and humorously that my real problem is me.

Now, two years after that bungled prayer, I continue to use it as a tool—kind of an inside joke between me and my Higher Power. It reminds me that all of those "defective characters" are his children, too, and probably not as bad as I make them out to be.

Anonymous, November 1998

Blackboard Wisdom
From Kingman, Arizona:

I'D LIKE TO PASS ALONG an anonymous thought I saw written on a blackboard at an AA meeting: "If you have to take ten minutes to justify what you said in five, you are probably full of it."

Ray G., December 1996

Exercise—Spiritual and Otherwise
From Palm Harbor, Florida:

THE SERENITY PRAYER has been one of my loves since I first became sober. I took the first part of the prayer so literally that I sat or slept through my first five years of sobriety, although always attending meetings and listening and sharing and trying to carry the message.

Although I must remember the first part of the prayer, I've recently launched into the second, deeper part: "Courage to change the things I can."

I'm retired USAF and once had a good, muscular body; I could hike, camp, chop wood, and tramp on deer trails while on fishing trips. As the drinking got to the alcoholic stages, I quit everything for the booze. Then came retirement—and more booze and the rocker.

In sobriety, I realized that my body had become limp from lack of exercise, and I blamed it on arthritis. Exercise did hurt my joints, but now I've begun to do some walking and swimming, and I am toning those muscles (at age sixty) so that I can enjoy this wonderful sober life.

Thank God I got into action. I was sick and tired of sitting in that rocking chair. I'm not old unless I want to think I am. Now I'm enjoying exercising, swimming—and keeping it simple.

J.M., April 1980

Fine Days in All Weathers
From Chalk River, Ontario:

WE ARE HAVING one of our unusual storms. Yesterday, everybody thought they would be wearing an Easter outfit, but if this weather continues today and tomorrow, it will be fur parkas, high boots, and northern Ontario mukluks (Indian-made and very warm). I can't understand why I should be so happy on a day like this. I can remember forgetting to pick up enough wine for a three-day holiday and just about going bananas. Here it is Good Friday, and I'm not even thinking about wine. The fridge contains food—a far cry from the old days. In fact, we didn't have a fridge; the bailiff had taken that along with the stove and washer. If anyone had told me to try AA, I would have laughed at them and said, "Who, me?"

But a miracle happened nine years ago, and I found myself at an AA meeting in Toronto. I didn't know my own phone number, but I knew I was in the right place. There were no more excuses.

I'm still learning how to be thankful. I must work on defects of character every morning. Slow down and smell the flowers—they will surely come to this beautiful valley soon, something to look forward to. Enjoy the phone calls from friends, as far away as Toronto.

I may even learn French. I have done something with my life, instead of complaining.

I owe it all to that day when a member of AA said to me, "Maybe you'd like to go to AA now." Thank God I said yes.

F.M., August 1977

HP at Your Disposal
From Nantucket, Massachusetts:

CALLED UPON OR NOT, HP is present. I was reminded of this with a noisy racket in my garbage disposal.

In my twentieth year of sobriety, having drunk for twenty years before that, I made a major step on my own behalf and bought a house. I had some financial help, and I had enough belief in myself to carry forward this mortgage business. It was a real act of faith.

As some of you know, you don't really own houses, they own you. So as it would happen, one of the first things to attend to was the plumbing, including the garbage disposal. I'd never had a disposal before and didn't know the normal sounds one makes, but I found mine to be very noisy and scary, and when the plumber came, I asked him to take a look at it. He was unperturbed: Shining his light into the depths and then reaching his hand down, he brought a chewed-up coin. That was the cause of the racket.

He held it up for me to see: Written on the coin were the words "You are not alone."

"I know where that's from," I said.

"You too?" he said.

"Yep," I said, "nineteen and a half years."

"Well, I've got seven," he said. "I wouldn't be alive if it weren't for the rooms of AA."

Whoever had this house before me must have been in them too, at least once.

Together, the plumber and I put the mangled coin over the door, where it will remind me every time I come and go that I am not alone.

Mara C., February 1998

Anywhere, U.S.A.
From Omaha, Nebraska:

I WORK PART-TIME at our central office, and I received a phone call the other day from a man in California who identified himself as an alcoholic. He said he'd been sober for five days and then started drinking again but was sober that day. He asked if I was an alcoholic as well and wondered if I'd answer a few questions. Did I go to meetings? Did I read the Big Book? Did I call my sponsor? Did I take it one day at a time? And I was in Omaha, Nebraska, right?

I answered all his questions and asked him why he was concerned. He told me he was checking up on what his sponsor told him; he wanted to make sure that AA was the same outside of California as well as in it!

So if you ever wonder how AA works in the rest of the country, you can always pick up the phone and call Anywhere, U.S.A.

Steve N., April 1998

No More Perfection
From St. Petersburg, Florida:

WHEN I WAS A CHILD, I was taught that anything short of perfection would incur divine displeasure. As a result I grew up inwardly inhibited and frustrated. In those formative years, I had no way of knowing that nature, as expressed in this universe, does not believe in, nor demand, perfection.

Flunking my college course for the ministry found me a ripe sucker for alcohol. Escape from my badly formed conscience, numbness for my nagging frustrations, and an entrance into a newfound world of carefree gaiety, soon proclaimed to the world at large that I was an ardent disciple of John Barleycorn. Then alcoholism took over completely.

Now, thanks to the Higher Power that motivates Alcoholics Anonymous, I have a sane and good conscience, and no fanatical delusions about perfection.

I wouldn't want perfection if I could have it, because in that case I'd cease to be an alcoholic—and then I would certainly miss my AA group!

Z.P., January 1955

Coming To Believe
From Oakland, California:

THE OTHER NIGHT, a friend and I were leading the beginners meeting down at the central office. This is a structured series of meetings, and since it was my second time through the series, I thought I knew all the instructions. But all at once this sentence loomed in print: "Explain the difference between religion and spirituality." I don't remember ever having seen that sentence before! It was like rereading a passage in the Big Book and seeing it for the first time. I gave some sort of answer about church and the Fellowship, and we went on to the next set of instructions. However, the incident bothered me more than I wanted to admit.

When I first came into AA, I was an agnostic—or that was the label I put on myself. I could not accept any formal religion or God. But my life was unmanageable, so I just sat there and listened. After twiddling my thumbs through the moment of silence at the beginning of our meeting for some months, I realized I could ask for strength, both for myself and for the people I cared for, so it wasn't wasted time anymore. This action gradually evolved into a feeling that I have a Higher Power. The word *God* is too concrete a word for what I feel, so I when I read or say the Serenity Prayer, "God" becomes "Higher Power" in my heart. I also change the tense of the Second Step in my mind. I am "coming to believe." All of this may explain what happened.

I woke up the Saturday morning following the beginners meeting with the answer absolutely clear: Religion was something taught me, acquired, an external experience, while spirituality welled up from within, and required no education, no Torah or Bible, no shaman or priest.

I believe my Higher Power led me to this explanation, as it was too clear and bright an idea for so early in the morning!

T. T., August 1992

Internal Restoration
From McAllen, Texas:

RECENTLY A STORM blew the roof off my two-story home, and the rain caused much destruction. I lived in a friend's vacant home for three months while the whole house was done over and the furniture was restored. I jokingly said in a meeting, "I wish I could be restored, too!" Then that precious voice within me said, "What do you think has been happening to you these past thirty-five years?"

I'll be eighty years old on my next birthday. My husband died of cancer fifteen years ago; I had cancer of the mouth, a knee was replaced, a torn tendon was repaired, and a tumor was removed in my abdomen. But through it all, I was able to share at meetings how God took these crises in my life and turned them for good. Our strength is in our need for each other—from our Higher Power.

Few of us will ever be famous, but we can all be great because we serve each other.

Sue F., October 1997

Each One Counts
From Seattle, Washington:

I DOUBT VERY MUCH there is a single one of us on our way through the years who does not leave some faint imprint of his creative thinking, some meaningful expression, some small inspired insight as an addition to our healing body of thought. And each contribution is the life-stuff of the AA program. Ours is a living program.

H.S., June 1955

God grant me the serenity

to accept the things I cannot change,

courage to change the things I can,

and wisdom to know the difference.

1. We admitted we were powerless over alcohol—that our lives had become unmanageable.

2. Came to believe that a Power greater than ourselves could restore us to sanity.

3. Made a decision to turn our will and our lives over to the care of God <u>as we understood Him</u>.

4. Made a searching and fearless moral inventory of ourselves.

5. Admitted to God, to ourselves, and to another human being the exact nature of our wrongs.

6. Were entirely ready to have God remove all these defects of character.

7. Humbly asked Him to remove our shortcomings.

8. Made a list of all persons we had harmed, and became willing to make amends to them all.

9. Made direct amends to such people wherever possible, except when to do so would injure them or others.

10. Continued to take personal inventory and when we were wrong promptly admitted it.

11. Sought through prayer and meditation to improve our conscious contact with God <u>as we understood Him</u>, praying only for knowledge of His will for us and the power to carry that out.

12. Having had a spiritual awakening as the result of these steps, we tried to carry this message to alcoholics, and to practice these principles in all our affairs.

THE TWELVE TRADITIONS

1. Our common welfare should come first; personal recovery depends upon A.A. unity.

2. For our group purpose there is but one ultimate authority—a loving God as He may express Himself in our group conscience. Our leaders are but trusted servants; they do not govern.

3. The only requirement for A.A. membership is a desire to stop drinking.

4. Each group should be autonomous except in matters affecting other groups or A.A. as a whole.

5. Each group has but one primary purpose—to carry its message to the alcoholic who still suffers.

6. An A.A. group ought never endorse, finance or lend the A.A. name to any related facility or outside enterprise, lest problems of money, propert, and prestige divert us from our primary purpose.

7. Every A.A. group ought to be fully self-supporting, declining outside contributions.

8. Alcoholics Anonymous should remain forever nonprofessional, but our service centers may employ special workers.

9. A.A., as such, ought never be organized; but we may create service boards or committees directly responsible to those they serve.

10. Alcoholics Anonymous has no opinion on outside issues; hence the A.A. name ought never be drawn into public controversy.

11. Our public relations policy is based on attraction rather than promotion; we need always maintain personal anonymity at the level of press, radio and films.

12. Anonymity is the spiritual foundation of all our traditions, ever reminding us to place principles before personalities.

The AA Grapevine Statement of Purpose

THE AA GRAPEVINE is the international journal of Alcoholics Anonymous. Written, edited, illustrated, and read by AA members and others interested in the AA program of recovery from alcoholism, the Grapevine is a lifeline linking one alcoholic to another.

Widely known as a "meeting in print," the AA Grapevine communicates the experience, strength, and hope of its contributors and reflects a broad geographic spectrum of current AA experience with recovery, unity, and service. Founded in 1944, the Grapevine does not receive group contributions, but is supported entirely through magazine subscription sales and additional income derived from the sale of Grapevine items.

The awareness that every AA member has an individual way of working the program permeates the pages of the Grapevine, and throughout its history the magazine has been a forum for the varied and often divergent opinions of AAs around the world. Articles are not intended to be statements of AA policy, nor does publication of any article imply endorsement by either AA or the Grapevine.

As Bill W. expressed it in 1946, "The Grapevine will be the voice of the Alcoholics Anonymous movement. Its editors and staff will be primarily accountable to the AA movement as a whole. . . . Within the bounds of friendliness and good taste, the Grapevine will enjoy perfect freedom of speech on all matters directly pertaining to Alcoholics Anonymous. . . . Like the Alcoholics Anonymous movement it is to mirror, there will be but one central purpose: The Grapevine will try to carry the AA message to alcoholics and practice the AA principles in all its affairs."

Alcoholics Anonymous

AA'S PROGRAM of recovery is fully set forth in its basic text, *Alcoholics Anonymous* (commonly known as the Big Book), now in its Fourth Edition, as well as *Twelve Steps and Twelve Traditions* and other books. Information on AA can also be found on AA's website at www.aa.org or by writing to: Alcoholics Anonymous, Box 459, Grand Central Station, New York, NY 10163. For local resources, check your local telephone directory under "Alcoholics Anonymous."

The AA Grapevine

THE GRAPEVINE is AA's international monthly journal, published continuously since its first issue in June 1944. The AA pamphlet on the Grapevine describes its scope and purpose this way: "As an integral part of Alcoholics Anonymous for almost sixty years, the Grapevine publishes articles that reflect the full diversity of experience and thought found within the AA Fellowship. No one viewpoint or philosophy dominates its pages, and in determining content, the editorial staff relies on the principles of the Twelve Traditions."

In addition to a monthly magazine, the Grapevine also produces anthologies, audiocassette tapes, and audio CDs based on published articles, and an annual wall calendar and pocket planner.

For more information on the Grapevine, or to subscribe, please visit the magazine's website www.aagrapevine.org *or write:*

The AA Grapevine
475 Riverside Drive
New York, NY 10115

For subscription information call: (212) 870-3404
E-mail: gvcirculation@aagrapevine.org

Steps Copyright © AA World Services, Inc; reprinted with permission.

A Note from the Editors:

The conversation continues every month in
the Letters to the Editor section of the AA Grapevine,
PO Box 1980, and on the i-Say bulletin board
of the magazine's website — www.aagrapevine.org

We invite you to participate.

THIS BOOK IS SET IN COCHIN, a typeface produced by the French designer Georges Peignot (1872–1914), and based on the eighteenth century copper engravings of Charles Nicolas Cochin (1715–1790). Charles Malin cut the typeface in 1912 for the Paris foundry, Deberny & Peignot. It was very popular in the early 20th century. In 1977, British type designer Matthew Carter expanded this historic form. Cochin is especially large and wide, making it an easily readable text face.